MY AWESOME FIELD GUIDE
TO ROCKS & MINERALS

My Awesome

FIELD GUIDE to

ROCKS & MINERALS

Track and Identify Your Treasures

GARY LEWIS

ROCKRIDGE PRESS

Interior and Cover Designer: Joshua Moore
Photo Art Director/Art Manager: Michael Hardgrove
Editor: Orli Zuravicky
Production Editor: Ashley Polikoff
Front cover photography © iStock/Katarzyna Bialasiewicz and Shutterstock/vvoe.
Back cover photography © Ja Het/Shutterstock.
Interior photography used under license from Shutterstock.com; iStock.com; creativemarket.com and Alamy.com.

ISBN: Print 978-1-64152-595-4 | eBook 978-1-64152-873-3
R0

To my amazing wife, Jen,
who puts up with
my geology passion,
and to my children
(Fiona, Jemma, Madeline,
and Oliver) all of whom
have been dragged
around looking for rocks
and minerals.

Contents

WELCOME, ROCK HOUNDS! IX

ROCK HOUNDS ROCK!
(AND SO DOES THE EARTH!) 1

The Science of the Earth 2
Let's Dig into Minerals..................................... 6
Let's Dig into Rocks 18

HUNTING FOR TREASURES 27

Where to Hunt for Treasures 28
How to Use This Field Guide............................ 31
How to Identify Your Treasures 35
Tips on How to Organize Your Collection at Home 43

MINERALS 47

Silver	48	Gypsum	62
Arsenopyrite	49	Kaolinite	63
Marcasite	50	Alabaster	64
Molybdenite	51	Barite	64
Stibnite	52	Dolomite	65
Galena	52	Aragonite	65
Platinum	53	Wollastonite	66
Wolframite	53	Tremolite	66
Mercury	54	Opal	67
Chalcopyrite	54	Plagioclase	68
Pyrite	55	Milky Quartz	68
Pyrrhotite	56	Sillimanite	69
Gold	57	Beryl	69
Copper	58	Olivine	70
Bismuth	59	Amphibole	71
Feldspar	60	Pyroxene	72
Mica	61	Talc	73

Cummingtonite 73
Apatite 74
Actinolite 75
Diopside 75
Nephrite 76
Amazonite 76
Jadeite 77
Emerald 77
Epidote 78
Chlorite 79
Malachite 79
Kyanite 80
Sodalite 81
Labradorite 81
Aquamarine 82
Sapphire 82
Covellite 83
Azurite 83
Turquoise 84
Crocidolite 84
Rhodochrosite 85
Rose Quartz 85
Orthoclase 86
Amethyst 87
Bornite 87
Citrine 88
Amber 88
Siderite 89
Topaz 90
Diamond 91
Sulfur 92
Biotite 93
Tourmaline 94
Augite 95
Hornblende 95

Jet 96
Chromite 96
Graphite 97
Ilmenite 97
Magnetite 98
Pyrolusite 98
Hematite 99
Quartz 100
Calcite 101
Selenite 102
Muscovite 103
Herkimer Diamond 103
Halite 104
Ulexite 104
Cerussite 105
Anorthoclase 105
Fluorite 106
Tiger's Eye 107
Agate 108
Andalusite 108
Flint 109
Cassiterite 110
Smoky Quartz 110
Staurolite 111
Corundum 111
Sphalerite 112
Goethite 112
Rutile 113
Cuprite 114
Titanite 114
Garnet 115
Zircon 115
Ruby 116
Realgar 116
Cinnabar 117

ROCKS 119

Granite 120
Tonalite 120
Monzonite 121
Pegmatite 121
Porphyry 122
Granodiorite 122
Syenite 123
Diorite 123
Gabbro 124
Peridotite 124
Carbonatite 125
Picrite 125
Ignimbrite 126
Scoria 127
Pyroclastic 127
Andesite 128
Trachyte 128
Tuff 129
Dacite 130
Basalt 130
Pumice 131
Rhyolite 131
Obsidian 132
Conglomerate 133
Breccia 133

Oil Shale 134
Graywacke 134
Shale 135
Sandstone 135
Diatomite 136
Chert 136
Limestone 137
Oolite 137
Chalk 138
Laterite 138
Anthracite 139
Lignite 139
Banded Iron Formation .. 140
Bauxite 140
Gneiss 141
Amphibolite 141
Migmatite 142
Schist 143
Marble 144
Quartzite 145
Hornfels 145
Slate 146
Phyllite 146
Serpentinite 147
Soapstone 147

MY FIELD NOTEBOOK 149

How to Use This Notebook 150

Glossary 207

Fact Sheets Index 211

Index 214

Welcome, Rock Hounds!

Have you ever wanted to be a treasure hunter? Now you can be! My name is Gary, and I've been collecting **rocks** and **minerals** since I was your age. I had so much fun collecting that I became a **geologist**—a scientist who studies the Earth's physical features, especially its rocks and minerals! Now I travel the world looking for rocks and minerals to add to my collection. You can be a treasure hunter just like me! There's even a name for treasure hunters like you: **rock hounds**. Rock hounds have a passion for collecting rocks and minerals but may not have studied them like geologists do.

It's really easy to get started rock hounding. With this awesome guide, you will learn how to collect samples and how to identify your rock and mineral treasures; and, with over 150 rock and mineral fact sheets chock-full of information, you'll learn all about your treasures! You'll even learn how to store them and record notes about them. And the best part is that you can start collecting right in your own neighborhood! I hope that you enjoy using this guide and that you end up loving rocks and minerals as much as I do.

Let's get treasure hunting!

Rock Hounds Rock! (And So Does the Earth!)

Imagine how cool it would be if you were a treasure hunter. You could collect your treasure from amazing places and display it for everyone to see. You could have shiny gems, exotic minerals, and rare **crystals**. You could have rocks that came from famous places or even from outer space! And each of those treasures could tell a story—of where you found it, how you found it, or why it was so important that you have it in your collection.

WELL, YOU *CAN* DO all of those things, and I'm going to show you how. But first, let's talk science!

The Science of the Earth

Before we start to learn about the Earth and its rocks and minerals, we need to talk about the **chemistry**, or makeup, of "things." Everything we have ever known, touched, smelled, eaten, and played with is made up of **chemicals**. Those chemicals are made up of different chemical **elements** that are all linked together. "Element" is the term for the smallest chemical building block. There are around 118 known elements, and they can link together in many different combinations to form an almost unlimited variety of chemicals. Some of those elements are very common on the Earth, like silicon, oxygen, and aluminum, and some are very rare, like gold, silver, and platinum. A good collection contains a mix of rocks and minerals that are made up of both common and rare elements.

Cape Dyrhólaey, Iceland

LET'S TALK ABOUT SCIENTISTS

A geologist is a type of scientist (like me) who is trained to understand rocks and minerals and how they make up the Earth and other planets. This science is called **geology**. Geologists also study how those rocks are formed (including volcanoes), how rocks are worn away, and how their minerals can be washed out to sea by mighty rivers. Geologists also study natural disasters like earthquakes, tsunamis, and landslides. They are scientists who really help us understand how our planet works.

Some special geologists study minerals, crystals, and gems. They are called mineralogists or gemologists. They study how to identify minerals and gems, and the rocks in which they are found. Scientists who study the chemistry of rocks and minerals are called **geochemists**.

All of these scientists know that rocks and minerals change from place to place. But every new place is a new adventure just waiting to be explored!

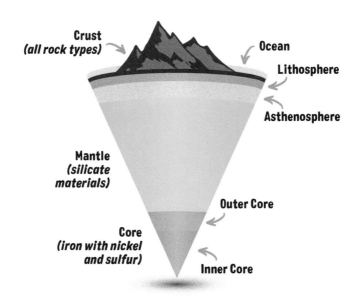

Crust
(all rock types)

Ocean

Lithosphere

Asthenosphere

Mantle
(silicate
materials)

Outer Core

Core
(iron with nickel
and sulfur)

Inner Core

THE LAYERS OF THE EARTH

The Earth is made up of layers of rocks, sort of like an onion. The layer that we all experience is called the **crust**. We find all of our rocks and minerals in this outer layer. The crust contains all three of the major rock groups: **igneous**, **sedimentary**, and **metamorphic**. But the other two layers of the Earth play an important role in what we find, too.

Deep below the crust is the thickest layer of the Earth, called the **mantle**. The rocks of the mantle are very hot—400 degrees Fahrenheit (200 degrees Celsius) to around 7,000 degrees Fahrenheit (3,800 degrees Celsius)—are under great pressure, and can flow. The mantle is *not* **molten** (or so hot that it's liquid), but some pockets of the mantle can become so hot that they melt and cause rocks in the overlying crust to also melt.

Below the mantle are the Earth's **core** layers—the outer core. The core is very hot—6,000 degrees Fahrenheit (3,300 degrees Celsius). The outer core is liquid, but the pressure of all the rocks on top of it keep the inner core solid.

The crust—the part of the Earth we all live on—is actually very thin. In some places it is just a few miles (5 to 10 kilometers) thick, like in the deep ocean basins. In other places, like at mountain ranges, the crust is many tens of miles (40 to 60 kilometers) thick. One other very important thing to know about the crust is that it is not sitting still. It's moving! Very slowly, but in your lifetime, it will move around 10 to 20 feet (3 to 7 meters) or more. And it's not moving all at the same speed and in all the same directions. In fact, the Earth's crust is broken up into slabs that geologists call **plates**. All of these plates are moving slowly in different directions. The places where the plates meet are called **plate boundaries**, and those are where most of the Earth's earthquakes happen and volcanoes are located. They can also be places where huge mountain ranges are formed and molten rock is squeezed up deep into the crust to cool slowly over time. But crazily, over millions of years, these plate boundaries can change. Often, these old plate boundary places are also some great locations for collecting mineral and rock **specimens**.

Let's Dig into Minerals

All the rocks in all the layers are made up of a mixture of different minerals clumped together. Minerals are the building blocks for our planet. To understand our planet, you have to understand those building blocks. You might be wondering, "What exactly *is* a mineral, anyway?" A scientist will say a mineral is "a naturally occurring, inorganic solid that has a definite chemical composition and whose atoms are arranged in an ordered fashion." That definition includes a lot of fancy words, but what does it *really* mean? Let's look at each part separately to understand it.

→ **Naturally occurring** means that it is not made by humans.

→ **Inorganic** means that it was not made by animals or plants and has never been alive.

→ **Solid** means it is not a liquid (like water or milk) or a gas (like air).

→ **Definite chemical composition** means that it has a known makeup of different chemical elements.

→ **Arranged in an ordered fashion** means that those chemical elements are joined together in a regular pattern, mostly to form crystals (even if they are so small that we can't see them).

HOW MINERALS ARE FORMED

Minerals form when the Earth's elements are combined through some normal Earth processes, like melting, weathering, or cooking (also called **metamorphism**). (We'll discuss this more in the rock section!) The mineral that forms depends on the elements that are available. Elements will arrange themselves in a pattern that is stable at the time of formation. Some minerals are stable at very high temperatures and under very high pressure, like diamonds. Others are stable at low temperatures and low pressure, like opals. When minerals form, the stability of elements plays a role in what the mineral becomes. That means if a rock is forming at very high temperatures deep in the Earth's crust, the minerals that form will be ones that can form in those conditions. Sometimes, when those minerals are brought up to the surface, their elements will want to rearrange over many years into a different mineral that is stable at low temperature and low pressure.

BREAKING DOWN MINERALS

Identifying specimens is a little like detective work, as many minerals can look the same. But if you know the mineral's characteristics—we geologists call them "properties"—you can sort out what mineral you have. Here is the list of mineral properties used in this guide and found on each mineral fact sheet. You'll use some of them to help you identify a mystery mineral you've found, and others will help you learn more about a specimen once you know what it is. One *big* secret here is that you *must* not use only one property to identify (ID) a mineral; you need to find two or more to be certain of what you have!

COLOR

It may seem odd, but color is often *not* a good way to identify a mineral, as many minerals can have many different colors. Still, color is normally one of the first things we can plainly see when we find a mystery mineral. For that reason, we use color in this book as the property to get you started on identifying your minerals. But always keep in mind that you need more than color to make a correct identification (ID)!

LUSTER

Luster is the way that light bounces off a mineral and how the mineral looks to us. "Metallic" means that a specimen looks like a metal, and "vitreous" means a specimen looks glossy like a glass.

HARDNESS

Minerals have different hardness levels. These levels are measured using the Mohs Scale of Hardness—a scale where ten of the most common minerals are given a number from softest to hardest. Hardness is one of the properties you will use to ID your minerals. Use Mohs Scale to work out the hardness of a mineral you are trying to ID.

MOHS SCALE OF HARDNESS
(from softest to hardest)

Talc	1
Gypsum	2
Calcite	3
Fluorite	4
Apatite	5
Orthoclase	6
Quartz	7
Topaz	8
Sapphire (Corundum)	9
Diamond	10

CLEAVAGE AND FRACTURE

Cleavage is the way a mineral will break to form a flat surface. Some minerals have perfect cleavage, which means that they want to break to form a smooth surface. Others leave rough surfaces. **Fracture** is what a mineral does if you try to break it against its cleavage—sort of like when you break a bone: It can break cleanly, or it can fracture in a more complicated way. Some minerals have curved fracture, like glass and quartz.

Specific gravity is how heavy a mineral is. It is measured in how many grams (g or gms) are in one unit of volume (a cubic centimeter or cc). The larger the number, the heavier it is!

Streak is the color of the powdered mineral. It can be very different from the color of the hard, formed mineral. This is one of the important properties you will use to ID minerals.

All minerals seem to form crystals in different ways. We call these **habits**. Examples of some of these are cubes or six-sided crystals. Some minerals just form clumps, which we call **massive**. Sometimes a crystal grows next to and joined to the same mineral. This is called **twinning**.

This is the chemical formula or code used by scientists to write down the elements that make up the mineral. Each element has its own code. Codes can be one capital letter (like O for oxygen) or a capital letter with a second letter (like Si for silicon).

All the elements and their codes are listed in a special table called the periodic table of the elements (on pages 12-13).

All the minerals of the world can be placed into about five major groups. Geochemists may break those down into even more groups, but for our purposes we'll concentrate on these major five.

SILICATES

These are the major **rock forming minerals**, and they make up almost all the rocks that we find in the Earth. These include quartz, olivine, talc, emerald, garnet, feldspar, mica, clays, and so many more. (Read more about silicates in the sidebar on page 14.)

NATIVE ELEMENTS

These are minerals that are made up of just *one* element such as gold, silver, copper, and sulfur. The element carbon can also be found as a native element, but its mineral name is diamond or graphite. Native elements are quite rare.

SULFIDES AND FRIENDS

These are minerals that contain sulfur as one of their elements. These include many of the metal-looking minerals like pyrite, bornite, galena, and chalcopyrite.

OXIDES AND FRIENDS

These are minerals that contain oxygen as one of the main elements, along with some related minerals. Minerals like hematite and rutile fall into this group, and so does the mineral halite, which is the salt that you put on your food and use on snowy

PERIODIC TABLE

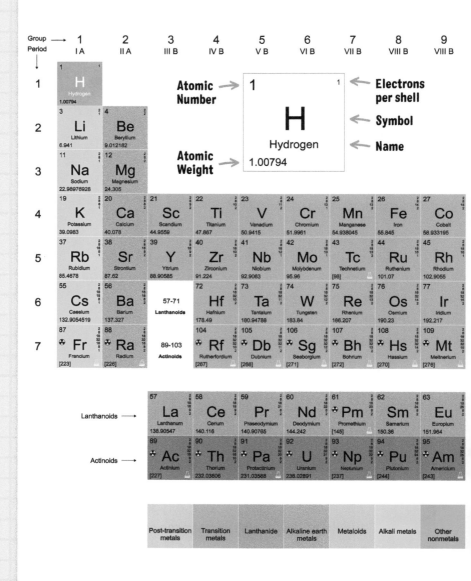

OF ELEMENTS

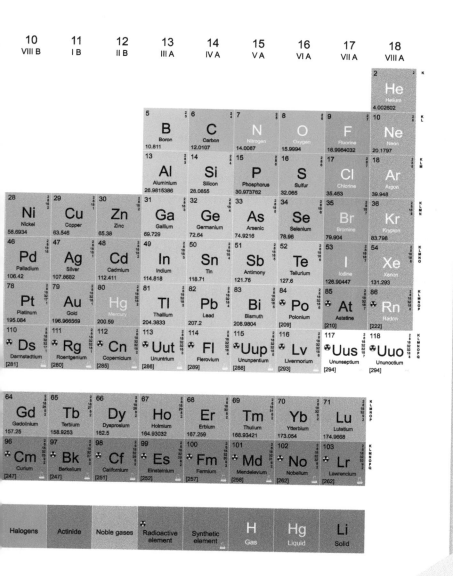

10 VIII B	11 I B	12 II B	13 III A	14 IV A	15 V A	16 VI A	17 VII A	18 VIII A
								2 He Helium 4.002602
			5 B Boron 10.811	6 C Carbon 12.0107	7 N Nitrogen 14.0087	8 O Oxygen 15.9994	9 F Fluorine 18.9984032	10 Ne Neon 20.1797
			13 Al Aluminium 26.9815386	14 Si Silicon 28.0855	15 P Phosphorus 30.973762	16 S Sulfur 32.065	17 Cl Chlorine 35.453	18 Ar Argon 39.948
28 Ni Nickel 58.6934	29 Cu Copper 63.546	30 Zn Zinc 65.38	31 Ga Gallium 69.729	32 Ge Germanium 72.64	33 As Arsenic 74.9216	34 Se Selenium 78.96	35 Br Bromine 79.904	36 Kr Krypton 83.798
46 Pd Palladium 106.42	47 Ag Silver 107.8682	48 Cd Cadmium 112.411	49 In Indium 114.818	50 Sn Tin 118.71	51 Sb Antimony 121.76	52 Te Tellurium 127.6	53 I Iodine 126.90447	54 Xe Xenon 131.293
78 Pt Platinum 195.084	79 Au Gold 196.966569	80 Hg Mercury 200.59	81 Tl Thallium 204.3833	82 Pb Lead 207.2	83 Bi Bismuth 208.9804	84 Po Polonium [209]	85 At Astatine [210]	86 Rn Radon [222]
110 Ds Darmstadtium [281]	111 Rg Roentgenium [280]	112 Cn Copernicium [285]	113 Uut Ununtrium [286]	114 Fl Flerovium [289]	115 Uup Ununpentium [288]	116 Lv Livermorium [293]	117 Uus Ununseptium [294]	118 Uuo Ununoctium [294]

64 Gd Gadolinium 157.25	65 Tb Terbium 158.9253	66 Dy Dysprosium 162.5	67 Ho Holmium 164.93032	68 Er Erbium 167.259	69 Tm Thulium 168.93421	70 Yb Ytterbium 173.054	71 Lu Lutetium 174.9668
96 Cm Curium [247]	97 Bk Berkelium [247]	98 Cf Californium [251]	99 Es Einsteinium [252]	100 Fm Fermium [257]	101 Md Mendelevium [258]	102 No Nobelium [262]	103 Lr Lawrencium [262]

Halogens	Actinide	Noble gases	Radioactive element	Synthetic element	H Gas	Hg Liquid	Li Solid

SILICATES

Silicate minerals are made up of the elements silicon and oxygen, which are joined together to form a strong, pyramid-shaped block. These blocks are then joined to form basic shapes, which give those minerals their properties, especially the way they cleave or fracture.

Single blocks: These minerals have one block surrounded by elements like iron and magnesium.

Double blocks: These minerals have two blocks joined together surrounded by elements like iron and magnesium.

Rings: These minerals have blocks joined together to form rings, and the rings are joined together through other elements.

Chains: These minerals form from long chains of blocks joined together by other elements.

Sheets: These minerals form great sheets of blocks.

Framework: These minerals form great frameworks of blocks.

roads in winter. (But please don't try to eat road salt—it is not pure enough for eating!) Many ore minerals, like iron ore and aluminum ore, are oxide minerals.

CARBONATES AND FRIENDS

These are minerals that contain the elements carbon and oxygen as their major elements, along with some related minerals. These are common minerals like calcite and dolomite.

MORE ABOUT MINERALS

WHAT IS A GEMSTONE?

Some minerals are cut and polished and used for making jewelry and ornaments. These are called **gemstones**, or even just **gems**. Often, they are divided up into **precious** (very rare) and **semi-precious** (not as rare).

QUARTZ VEINS AND BLOWS

The mineral quartz is the major mineral that makes up **veins** in the Earth. Veins are long, often thin layers of once-molten rock that has been squeezed into the cracks of existing rocks and cooled. Quartz veins can be found almost any-where on our planet—and can range in size from almost microscopic veins to ones that are as thick as houses. Because quartz does not weather away into another mineral and is quite hard, it often makes obvious features in the landscape: great white lines and round outcrops called blows.

SKIN DEEP

Some minerals are found as coatings on the outside of their host mineral. It may be that the host mineral is weathering away to form the new mineral, or that the host mineral reacted chemi-cally in the past to passing ore fluids. But those coatings can be spectacular! They can be shiny (metallic), colorful, and even sparkly (drusy).

HOLES, VUGS, AND SPACES

For larger, well-formed crystals to grow, they need a space to grow into. You may find spaces with crystals growing into the center, which are called **vugs**. Often, the vug has been filled with hot mineral-rich water from which the crystals have grown, and then the water has drained away.

GEODES

A special type of vug is known as a geode. They are normally round-shaped and, when cracked open,

Amethyst Geode

can be full of small crystals of minerals—most often quartz, which changes from white or clear to purple amethyst. But geodes can also be full of layers of minerals so that they look like stripes.

GOLD AND FOOL'S GOLD

Gold is one of the most sought-after of all the minerals. It is also very easy to identify. However, many other minerals can fool people into thinking they have found gold. The most important thing to remember is that gold is *very* heavy. It is also soft, and its streak is *always* gold. All the other "fool's gold" minerals do not have those properties.

FOSSILS AND MINERALS

Fossils are the preserved remains of plants and animals that are found inside of rocks. Often those remains are replaced by minerals, which can make the find even more spectacular. You can find fossils replaced by opal, calcite, quartz, and even pyrite.

Let's Dig into Rocks

Our planet is often referred to as a rocky planet because it is made almost completely of rocks. The only real exception is the water that fills our rivers, lakes, and oceans, and the thin layer of air that makes up our atmosphere. The rest is rock!

So, what exactly *is* a rock? A **rock** is a naturally occurring solid clump of minerals. The way those minerals are clumped can provide us with evidence on *how* that rock formed, and the types of minerals can tell us *where* it may have formed. We have three major groups of rocks: **igneous** rocks, which form from the cooling of molten material; **metamorphic** rocks, which form from the heat and/or high pressure from being underground; and **sedimentary** rocks, which are made up of fragments of rocks and minerals and are cemented together on the floors of lakes and oceans.

WHAT IS THE ROCK CYCLE?

Rocks are constantly being recycled. They are formed from molten or igneous rocks, then cooked up to form metamorphic rocks, which can be broken down into fragments and washed into lakes and the ocean to form sedimentary rocks. They can be cooked again and even remelted to form new igneous rocks. This is known as the **rock cycle**. Our planet recycles the top layer of rocks over and over and over again. Most of the time, this is a slow process, and we humans don't even

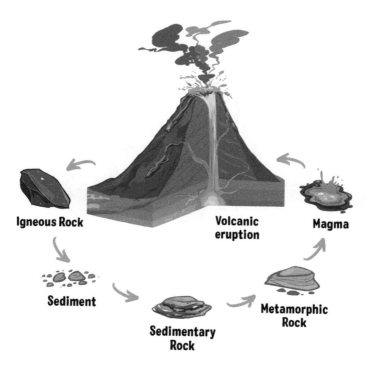

Igneous Rock

Volcanic eruption

Magma

Sediment

Sedimentary Rock

Metamorphic Rock

notice it. At other times, huge changes take place in the rocks around us like in landslides, floods, or volcanic eruptions. But over millions and millions of years, our planet has been changing the rocks around us, creating new and exciting minerals and destroying others.

BREAKING DOWN ROCKS

Rocks also have some easy-to-see characteristics that can be used to identify what you find in the field. These include color, the minerals the rocks contain, the size of grains and crystals, and even hardness. Sometimes you will see that one mineral in a rock is much larger than all the others. These

WEATHERING

Weathering is the process where rocks and minerals are changed due to the action of water, wind, or air at the Earth's surface. Sometimes this is just **mechanical**, which means that rocks and minerals are broken up into smaller pieces. Sand in a river or on the beach is the result of mechanical weathering. Sometimes weathering is **chemical**, which means that rocks and minerals change because the minerals react and **rot** with the water or air, changing into new minerals. Most of the time these new minerals are not very exciting to collect. But in other cases, chemical weathering can produce beautiful new minerals.

kinds of rocks are sometimes called porphyries (pronounced por-frees). Porphyries are igneous rocks that form this way when one mineral has had time to grow before all the other minerals.

One of the most important things to know is where a rock specimen has come from. When you buy or trade a rock, knowing where it came from is very important. If the trader can't tell you where a rock is from, don't add it to your collection!

COMPOSITION

All rocks are made up of minerals. Most rocks are made up of at least three major minerals and a handful of minor, sometimes called secondary, minerals. Occasionally, a rock will be made up almost entirely of one mineral.

CLASSIFICATION

All rocks can be divided up into the three major rock groups: igneous, metamorphic, or sedimentary. We will try to classify the rocks you collect into these three groups as a first step in our ID process. Then, we may be able to classify the rocks even further based on other properties like grain size or the minerals they contain. Sometimes it will be hard to tell where a rock belongs, but that's okay!

COLOR

A rock can have an overall color, which is made up of a mix of its mineral colors. The best way to see this overall color is to hold a rock at arm's length and slightly blur your eyes. What color do you see?

Is it dark or light? Does it have a color that catches your eye, like gray, pink, white, or red?

GRAIN SIZE

Rocks can be divided into three categories of grain size: coarse, medium, and fine. Can you easily see individual grains? Coarse. Can you see the grains but might need a magnifying glass to see them better? Medium. Can you see no grains at all even with a magnifying glass? Fine. We will use this property to help us ID our rocks.

HARDNESS

Is the rock hard? Can you scratch it with a nail or another rock? Is it crumbly? There is no scale for rocks like there is for minerals, but some rocks are much softer than others.

ORIGIN

Most rocks will easily fall into a category, most likely either igneous or sedimentary. Some rocks will be slightly more complicated, which is why knowing the origin is very important. A metamorphic rock has been formed by an original rock being cooked and/or put under a lot of pressure so new minerals have formed. Knowing the original rock before it was metamorphosed can help you understand the history of that metamorphic rock.

All the rocks on the Earth can be split up into the three groups mentioned earlier, depending on how they formed. That is pretty amazing! With practice, you will be able to work out the group of each rock you pick up when you're out collecting. Most of the time it is easy to work out. Sometimes it can be a little harder. But solving these mysteries is exactly what makes rock collecting so much fun!

IGNEOUS

The first way rocks are formed is from the cooling down of molten rock. These rocks are called igneous rocks. Can you imagine how hot rock must have to be to become molten? Super hot! And the only place it can happen is deep in the crust of the Earth. We call that molten rock **magma**. Sometimes, that molten rock cools down slowly over time. As the molten rock cools, crystals of minerals form and grow. The slower and longer the rock cools, the larger the crystals will be. These crystals all end up growing into each other and forming a solid rock. The crystals are so big that we can see them and often identify all the different minerals using only our eyes. We call igneous rocks that have cooled slowly and have larger crystals **plutonic** igneous rocks. Sometimes, some of the magma works its way up and reaches the surface of the Earth. When the molten rock is above ground, we call it **lava**. Lava cools quickly, so when the crystals form, they are very small—so small that we might need a microscope to see them. We call these rocks **volcanic** igneous rocks. Sometimes the lava cools so fast that the minerals can't form at all, and we get left with volcanic glass. When we collect igneous rocks, the size of the crystals gives us a clue to how quickly or slowly it cooled.

Igneous rocks are also divided up into groups based on the minerals they contain. The main minerals to consider are quartz and feldspar. If an igneous rock contains quartz and feldspar, then it

Mount Bromo, Indonesia

is called a **felsic** igneous rock. These tend to be light in color (pale grays). If it has no quartz at all, it is called a **mafic** igneous rock. These tend to be dark in color (black and dark grays). Igneous rocks that fall in between are called **intermediate** igneous rocks. They tend to be medium colors (like medium gray).

SEDIMENTARY

Over vast amounts of time, all the rocks on the Earth break down and wear away to small rock or mineral pieces. We call those pieces **sediments**. Over time, all of these loose sediments can become hardened or even cemented together to form sedimentary rocks. There is also a special kind of sedimentary rock made from the remains of animal shells that we call limestone. Coal is another sedimentary rock that is made up of parts of plants.

METAMORPHIC

The final type of rocks are those that have been changed over time because they have been cooked or put under a huge amount of pressure—or both! Because the rocks change, we call these metamorphic rocks; "metamorph" means "to change." But here is an important secret you should know: Though the minerals in metamorphic rocks may have changed from their original rock, they have done so *without* melting!

Now it's time to dive into where to go hunting, how to collect your treasures, and how to identify them. Are you ready to go hunting?

Hunting for Treasures

To be an awesome rock hound, you first need to learn some new skills. But don't worry—everything you need to learn is right here! First, I'll show you some great places right around the corner from you to go hunting. Next, you'll learn how to identify some common rocks and minerals, and then I'll teach you some scientific tests you can conduct to help you ID your finds. After all that, you can read more about what you've collected in this guide's over 150 amazing rock and mineral specimen fact sheets. You'll also learn how to label your treasures and store them properly in order to protect them.

Where to Hunt for Treasures

We all know some places around the globe that are famous because of their rocks. The Grand Canyon in Arizona is famous because a river cut a deep valley through many layers of different rocks. Mt. St. Helens in Washington state is famous because it is a volcano that last erupted in 1980, and Devils Tower in Wyoming is famous because it once was molten rock that cooled slowly underground. But you don't have to live near those places to start being a rock hound! You can start with rocks and minerals right in your own backyard, neighborhood, school playground, or park.

Devils Tower, United States

ROCK HUNTING NEAR YOU

Here are some neat places where you might be able to collect great specimens for your collection. You should *always* first check whether you are allowed to collect in these places; many federal, state, or locally managed land will not allow you to remove any rocks or minerals. And remember: Always go with a responsible adult, be safe, and make sure your folks know exactly where you will be.

→ Local park

→ Beach

→ Rocks around coastline

→ Road cuttings

→ Your own backyard

→ Your driveway (if it has loose material)

→ Local stone masons (they might let you pick from their bins)

→ School playground

→ Road maintenance gravel dumps

→ River and creek banks

→ Forest paths

Put all the items listed here in your back pocket or a small bag, and you'll have a "rock hound kit" that you can take with you everywhere!

THINGS EVERY ROCK HOUND SHOULD ALWAYS CARRY

 → Pint-size, plastic sealable bags for specimens

 → Field notebook to record information (included in this book)

 → Specimen numbers to place with your specimens (also included in this book)

 → Folded paper towel to wrap up delicate minerals for safe keeping

 → This book—of course!

HANDY TOOLS FOR ROCK HUNTING TRIPS LONGER THAN 30 MINUTES

 → A map, compass, or GPS on a smart-phone to help you navigate

 → Larger bags for bigger specimens

 → Old toothbrushes and wooden tooth-picks for cleaning up samples a little

 → Hand lens or small foldable magnifying glass to help see smaller minerals (I use this tool a lot)

 → Empty egg cartons to place small samples in. Close the egg carton with a rubber band to protect your samples.

How to Use This Field Guide

This guide will help you be a rock and mineral detective while in the field. The first step to your detective work will be to use the field notebook in the back of this book (see page 149) to record your field data. Your field notebook provides all the important instructions you need to record your data correctly.

Once you've recorded your data and brought your treasures home, you'll be ready to identify what you've found. First, you'll write down some careful observations and perform simple tests. Once you've identified your treasure, you can read more about it in its detailed fact sheet.

And remember: Practice makes perfect. You'll probably make a few mistakes in the beginning, but you'll get better over time. The best rock hound is the one who has seen the most rocks!

READING A SPECIMEN FACT SHEET

This guide has mineral and rock fact sheets for over 150 of the most common treasures you will find and add to your collection. They are put in groups to make it easier for you to ID your finds. Check out the following sample fact sheets for tips on where to find all the information.

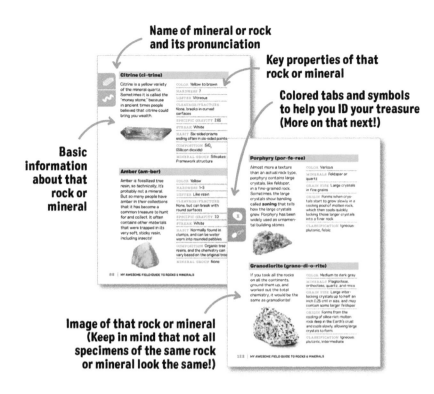

Name of mineral or rock and its pronunciation

Key properties of that rock or mineral

Colored tabs and symbols to help you ID your treasure (More on that next!)

Basic information about that rock or mineral

Image of that rock or mineral (Keep in mind that not all specimens of the same rock or mineral look the same!)

READING THE COLORED TABS AND SYMBOLS

To help you ID what you find in the field, each rock and mineral fact sheet has colored tabs with symbols that you will use during the identification process.

The background colors on the tabs indicate different sections of the book. Turquoise background tabs indicate the *mineral fact sheets* section; pink background tabs indicate the *rock fact sheets* section; and blue background tabs indicate the *field notebook* section.

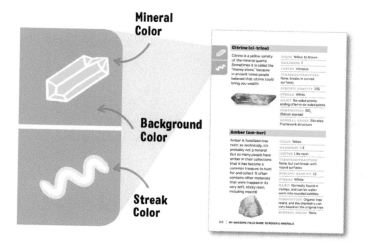

Mineral Color

Background Color

Streak Color

A small colored crystal on the tab of each mineral page shows you the most common color that each mineral forms. You will use this colored symbol to begin to help you ID your mineral. (But remember: We never use color alone to ID a mineral!)

A small colored squiggly line on the tab of each mineral page indicates the streak color that each mineral creates. You will also use this colored symbol to help you ID your mineral. (Some minerals have no streak; for these minerals, there will be no streak symbol on the tab.)

A small rock symbol with a capital letter on the tab of each rock page shows you what rock group each rock belongs to: I for igneous, S for sedimentary, or M for metamorphic. You will use these rock group symbols to help you ID your rock treasures.

Three small grain size symbols on the tab of each rock page show you the different grain sizes for each rock: the biggest is coarse, the middle is

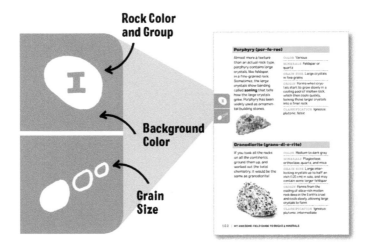

Rock Color and Group

Background Color

Grain Size

medium, or the smallest is fine. You will also use these grain size symbols to help you ID your rock treasures.

Remember to always check and double-check the properties you find for your mineral or rock sample. A good detective always has multiple facts to back up their conclusion, and as a rock hound detective, you should too!

HOW THE ROCKS AND MINERALS ARE ORGANIZED

The rock and mineral fact sheets are organized in a specific way to help you identify your mystery treasures. *Mineral fact sheets* are organized first by their mineral color and second by their streak color. Main colors are also broken up into metallic colors and nonmetallic colors. *Rock fact sheets* are organized first by the type of rock and second by their grain size (coarse, medium, fine).

→ There are some fact sheets that don't fit neatly into any of these categories, and those are placed at the end of each section.

→ There are also some minerals that fall into two color categories. These minerals have their main fact sheets listed under their most common color and shortened entries under secondary color for the most useful identification method.

How to Identify Your Treasures

Let's say you are treasure hunting in a nearby park, and you come across an unknown mineral you want to ID. You are now going to think like a detective. As you do your detective work, you'll use the notebook in this book to record the answers to some of the questions in the "Identifying Specimens" section coming up, as well as the results of the tests you'll perform.

Follow those steps to crack the case of what your mineral is!

WHAT YOU NEED

→ **An uncoated white tile.** You can get one from a big hardware store. A white glazed tile will often not be glazed on the back, so you can use it to check the streak of a mineral.

→ **A set of hardness testers.** See how to make your own set next.

→ **A magnifying glass or a hand lens.**
Use this to see the cleavage and luster of
small minerals.

→ **Some way to store your minerals once
you've brought them home.** As mentioned
earlier, egg cartons are great for small
minerals. Small boxes are great for larger
samples. Start collecting boxes from shoes
and other household items. Reuse and recycle!

→ **This book,** including the numbered specimens.

HOW TO MAKE YOUR OWN HARDNESS SCALE

One of the simple tests you can perform at home
to help you identify your treasures is to test their
hardness. You can do this by creating your very own
Mohs Scale of Hardness! Working out a mineral's
hardness compared to other known minerals might
seem like a hard thing to do, but the idea behind it is
pretty simple. Your goal is to see if the mystery
mineral you want to ID can scratch another mineral.
If it can, then your mineral is *harder* than that
mineral. If the other mineral scratches *your* mineral,
then your mineral is *softer* than that mineral.

There are some kits you can buy that have some
minerals to use for this job, but you can also make
your own test kit using some common objects.

Collect these items and keep them in a special
box or bag. If you find some minerals on the Mohs
Scale of Hardness (see page 9), you can add those
to your kit as well. Make sure you make up a list of

what your kit contains and each item's hardness so you can refer to your list when testing.

HARDNESS SCALE OF COMMON ITEMS

ITEM	HARDNESS
Fingernail	2
Copper coin	3
Scissor blade	5
Window glass	5.5
Metal nail file	6.5

(CAUTION: With all sharp and/or breakable items, be sure to have an adult help you with testing.)

Now you are ready to check the hardness of all the rocks and minerals you collect!

IDENTIFYING SPECIMENS

When you are ready to identify a specimen, your first task is to clean it! Most specimens will have some mud and/or dirt on them, and cleaning that off will make the specimen easier to identify. In almost every case, rinsing your specimen with water will be the best and simplest way to clean it. You could also use a soft, old toothbrush to loosen material, but be very careful if your specimen has lots of fine crystals, because you don't want to break any of them. A useful trick is to let your very dirty specimens soak for a few days—that will really help get them clean. Sometimes, you might need something stronger than just water. Believe it or not, a cola works very well to remove some stubborn dirt and stains from some minerals!

Once your specimen is clean, you have to make your very first big detective decision: Is your specimen a rock (a sample that contains lots of minerals all joined together, like granite or conglomerate) or a mineral (mostly one or two types of minerals in a clump, like quartz, pyrite, or chalcopyrite). Sometimes this is easy to work out. Other times, you might have something that falls in between. That's okay. It's fine to not be sure. Just remember to write what you think you have (rock or mineral) in the notebook section (see page 149).

STEPS FOR IDENTIFYING A MINERAL

1. Identify if your mineral is a metallic mineral or a nonmetallic mineral. Does it look like a metal? Many minerals do. (This feature is really a type of luster!) Once you determine if it's metallic or nonmetallic, you will then choose its closest color. The colors in the mineral fact sheets are listed as metallic or nonmetallic.

2. Next, record its color in the table on the notebook page for this specimen. Is it blue? Gray? Metallic yellow? Remember: We are only using color as our first property. Color alone will not give you a good ID!

3. Next, identify its streak color by performing the streak test: Scratch the mineral on an unglazed tile. Check that your specimen is not scratching the tile (the mineral needs to be *softer* than the tile for this to work). Record the color of the scratch in the table.

4. Measure your mineral's hardness by performing the Mohs Scale of Hardness test using the kit you made (see the section on page 36). Record your answer in the table.

Once you have done these tests, you can find the correct section of the mineral fact sheets by doing the following:

1. Turn to the mineral fact sheets by finding the turquoise colored tabs on the side of the pages. (See page 32 to refresh your memory on how to read this guide.)

2. Locate the correct mineral color section by finding the correct color mineral symbol on the tab.

3. Locate the correct color streak section by finding the correct color streak symbol on the tab.

4. Locate the mineral or minerals that have those properties *and* the right level of hardness you found during your test.

These tests might lead you to find a perfect match for your specimen. But you might also find that your specimen matches more than one mineral, in which case you need to look at even more properties, like cleavage/fracture and luster, to see if that narrows it down to one match. If you still can't find your mineral, it may be that it is not displaying its typical color; many minerals can have multiple colors, so you will need to look at other color possibilities in the fact sheets. This may take some time, but with practice you will become a great mineral collector.

STEPS FOR IDENTIFYING A ROCK

1. Identify the rock group it falls into: igneous, metamorphic, or sedimentary. Look at how the grains are shaped and how they are placed together. If you can see the grains, look for the following signs:

→ If you can see grains that look crystalline (meaning they have cleavage faces, are shiny, etc.) and the entire rock is similar in appearance (meaning there is no banding or layers), then the rock type will most likely be *igneous*.

→ If the grains look crystalline but the rock has layers or banding, then it is probably *metamorphic*.

→ If the grains don't look crystalline but instead look more rounded, like sand or pebbles, and they look like they are cemented together rather than growing into each other, then the rock is probably *sedimentary*.

If you can't see grains, look for these signs:

→ If you can easily scratch the rock with an iron nail, then it is probably *not* igneous.

→ If the rock looks shiny when you move it around in the light, then it is probably *metamorphic*.

→ If it is soft and not shiny, then it may be *sedimentary*.

→ If it is hard and not shiny, then it is probably *igneous*.

Record your findings in the table of the specimen's notebook page. You can confirm your findings by noting where you collected the rock and checking a geologic map of the area (or ask a parent to download an app for geological maps) that will tell you the type of rocks you can expect to find there.

2. The next step in identifying a rock is to determine its grain size. Can you see the grains or crystals? Record your findings in the table.

→ If they are larger than a corn kernel, then the rock is coarse grained.

→ If you can see grains but they are smaller than a corn kernel, then it's medium grained.

→ If you can't see any grains or crystals, then it is fine grained.

3. Next, record the rock's color in the table. Hold the rock at arm's length, and describe its overall color.

4. If it is a medium- or coarse-grained rock, can you identify minerals? Write down your observations.

→ Can you see any quartz? In a rock, quartz will be a gray, glassy-looking mineral with no flat surfaces.

→ Can you see any flaky mica? Does the rock have a lot of mica?

Once you have done these tests, you can find the right section of the rock fact sheets by doing the following:

1. Turn to the rock fact sheets with the pink colored tabs on the side of the pages. (See page 32 to refresh your memory on how to read this guide.)

2. Locate the correct rock group section by the rock group symbol on the tab.

3. Locate the correct grain size group within that section.

4. If the rock is medium- to coarse-grained, look at the typical minerals that you can find in those rocks and match the rock up with the minerals you have identified.

As with any minerals you find, sometimes it will be easy to identify a rock. Other times, you might end up having to search through the guide because your rock may not be the common form of that rock. Following this process and with practice, you will learn to become a great rock detective!

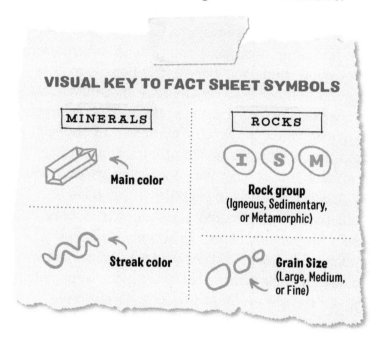

VISUAL KEY TO FACT SHEET SYMBOLS

MINERALS

Main color

Streak color

ROCKS

I S M

Rock group
(Igneous, Sedimentary,
or Metamorphic)

Grain Size
(Large, Medium,
or Fine)

Tips on How to Organize Your Collection at Home

Once you have taken all of your notes and identified your samples to the best of your ability, there are several ways to preserve the information and organize your collection of treasures. The first thing you can do (to make sure you never lose your notes) is to scan the notebook pages into a home computer. This way you will have your notes in a digital form and can organize them into folders or files on the computer in any way that works best for you. If this is not an option, be sure to always keep this book in a safe place where you can easily locate it. If you love being a rock hound, you will someday outgrow the notebook section in this book, so you should develop a labeling system for this and other notebooks you fill with information about your finds. You will want to be sure to note the last number used for the final specimen listed in one notebook so you can start the first specimen in a new notebook with the number that comes next. You don't want to end up with duplicate numbers; that will get very confusing, very quickly.

Now comes the fun part! When you have all your specimens at home, you'll want to display them for you and others to appreciate. Some people end up with a dedicated cabinet or place to display their treasures. Others place a specimen here and there around the house. It's entirely up to you.

If you choose to keep your treasures in one place, be sure to keep the numbers with the speci-mens—for your own purposes and for visitors who may drop by. There are several ways you can guide visitors to the information you've compiled about each specimen. You can create a list that simply states the numbers and the names and then directs people to a specific notebook for more information. Or, you can create a more detailed log

by typing up all of the information from your notebook. It's up to you!

If you choose to display your treasures (or some of them) separately, like I do, there are some things you can do to make your treasures nice for viewing. First, cut out a small pad of felt (or other cloth-like material) to go underneath each sample so it does not scratch the surface it sits on. You can then create a small label that has the name of the sample, where it comes from, the specimen number from your notebook, and the label number or name from the notebook the specimen is listed in. You can glue these to the material or write them on a separate card. My secret is to change around the specimens I display every once in a while. This adds some interest to people who visit *and* ensures that I get to enjoy all my samples!

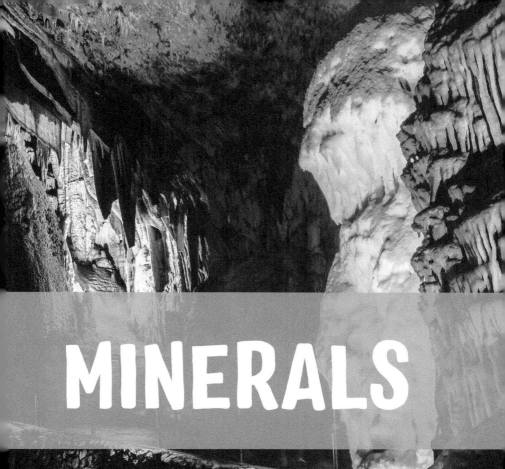

MINERALS

Silver (sil-ver)

Native silver is a rare find, but it can sometimes be found in veins with gold and other native metals. It mostly occurs as small clumps. It can also form in very delicate shapes, like wires and ferns, which might be stained black by other chemicals.

COLOR Metallic white

HARDNESS 2.5–3.0

LUSTER Metallic

CLEAVAGE/FRACTURE None

SPECIFIC GRAVITY 10–11

STREAK Silver

HABIT Normally massive, but can form wires, plates, etc.

COMPOSITION Ag (Silver)

MINERAL GROUP Native elements

Bismuth (bis-muth)

See full fact sheet on page 59.

Muscovite (mus-co-vite)

See full fact sheet on page 103.

Arsenopyrite (ar–se–no–pi–rite)

Arsenopyrite is often found with other sulfide minerals. It contains the element arsenic, which is poisonous in some forms! Arsenopyrite can contain gold and has been used as a gold ore in the past. Its crystals often have lots of small lines on them called striations. The crystals also can twin to form crosses and stars.

COLOR Metallic white

HARDNESS 5.5–6.0

LUSTER Metallic

CLEAVAGE/FRACTURE Good, in one direction

SPECIFIC GRAVITY 5.9–6.2

STREAK Black

HABIT Stubby crystals, often with striations

COMPOSITION FeAsS (Iron arsenic sulfide)

MINERAL GROUP Sulfides and friends

Marcasite (mar-ca-site)

Marcasite is often called white iron pyrite. It seems to have the same chemistry as pyrite, but it forms different types of crystals because the **atoms** are arranged in a different way. While marcasite can be found in veins along with pyrite and other sulfides, it is common to find this mineral in the sedimentary rocks shale and coal.

COLOR Metallic white

HARDNESS 6.0–6.5

LUSTER Metallic

CLEAVAGE/FRACTURE
Can cleave in one direction, but breaks unevenly

SPECIFIC GRAVITY 4.8

STREAK Black to gray

HABIT Tabular crystals, massive and spearhead twins

COMPOSITION FeS_2
(Iron sulfide)

MINERAL GROUP Sulfides and friends

Molybdenite (mo-lib-de-nite)

Molybdenite is an ore mineral of the metal molybdenum, which is used to make steel strong and resistant to rusting. Molybdenite has a strange, greasy texture that comes from the sheets of atoms inside it, which slide past each other. This mineral is found in high-temperature ore deposits along with pyrite and quartz. The largest deposits are found in Colorado's Rocky Mountains.

COLOR Gray

HARDNESS 1.0–1.5

LUSTER Metallic

CLEAVAGE/FRACTURE Perfect, forms sheets

SPECIFIC GRAVITY 4.73

STREAK Gray, with a bluish tinge

HABIT Forms thin, platy crystals, but also occurs as small grains with other sulfide minerals

COMPOSITION MoS_2 (Molybdenum sulfide)

MINERAL GROUP Sulfides and friends

Stibnite (stib-nite)

Stibnite is the major ore for a rare metal called antimony, so it is sometimes called antimonite. Stibnite is found with other ore minerals, including galena, pyrite, and arsenopyrite, and can form crystals inside of calcite or quartz. Stibnite is used in fireworks!

COLOR Gray

HARDNESS 2

LUSTER Metallic

CLEAVAGE/FRACTURE Good, in three directions

SPECIFIC GRAVITY 4.63

STREAK Gray

HABIT Forms needlelike crystals, often radiating from one point

COMPOSITION Sb_2S_3 (Antinomy sulfide)

MINERAL GROUP Sulfides and friends

Galena (ga-le-na)

Galena is a major ore of lead and can form beautiful, silver cubes. Galena is the official state mineral of Missouri and Wisconsin. Because of the lead, always be sure to wash your hands after you touch galena.

COLOR Gray

HARDNESS 2.50–2.75

LUSTER Metallic

CLEAVAGE/FRACTURE Forms perfect cubes, and can fracture unevenly

SPECIFIC GRAVITY 7.2–7.6

STREAK Lead gray

HABIT Forms cubes and eight-sided shapes

COMPOSITION PbS (Lead sulfide)

MINERAL GROUP Sulfides and friends

Platinum (plat–i–num)

Platinum is a rare native metal, often found mixed with iron, gold, copper, and other rare metals. These other metals make platinum seem lighter than it should be. When it contains a lot of iron, it can become magnetic. Platinum is often mistaken for native silver.

COLOR Gray

HARDNESS 4.0–4.5

LUSTER Metallic

CLEAVAGE/FRACTURE None, breaks unevenly

SPECIFIC GRAVITY 14–19

STREAK Silvery gray

HABIT Mostly found as water-worn nuggets, and rarely, crystals form cubes with rounded corners

COMPOSITION Pt (Platinum)

MINERAL GROUP Native elements

Wolframite (wol–fram–ite)

Wolframite is an ore mineral for the element tungsten. It is found in veins and pegmatites around granite bodies. It is often found with other minerals such as cassiterite and scheelite.

COLOR Gray

HARDNESS 4.0–4.5

LUSTER Metallic

CLEAVAGE/FRACTURE Perfect, in one direction

SPECIFIC GRAVITY 7.0–7.5

STREAK Reddish brown

HABIT Forms tabular or short, prism-shaped crystals

COMPOSITION $(Fe,Mn)WO_4$ (Iron/magnesium tungsten oxide)

MINERAL GROUP Oxides and friends

Mercury (mur-cu-ree)

Mercury is a liquid metal sometimes found around old gold processing plants. It was used by miners to separate gold from its crushed ore. It is a dangerous substance that should be collected by only professionals. If you think you've found it, don't touch it—just photograph it!

COLOR Gray

HARDNESS 0

LUSTER Metallic

CLEAVAGE/FRACTURE None

SPECIFIC GRAVITY 13.6

STREAK None

HABIT Droplets of liquid

COMPOSITION Hg (Mercury)

MINERAL GROUP Native elements

Chalcopyrite (chal-co-py-rite)

Chalcopyrite is a copper ore mineral that is often mistaken for pyrite. Chalcopyrite can be found in the same rock as pyrite, but it has a deeper yellow color. It can also be found with blue and green copper minerals on mine dumps or in veins.

COLOR Yellow

HARDNESS 3.5

LUSTER Metallic

CLEAVAGE/FRACTURE Poor, breaks unevenly

SPECIFIC GRAVITY 4.1–4.3

STREAK Black, with a greenish tinge

HABIT Mostly massive, but can form small crystals

COMPOSITION $CuFeS_2$ (Copper iron sulfide)

MINERAL GROUP Sulfides and friends

Pyrite (py-rite)

Pyrite, sometimes called iron pyrite, is mistaken for gold so often that it has been given the name "fool's gold." Pyrite is the most common sulfide mineral and can be found in veins, with other ore minerals, or even as a mineral making up some fossils. It smells of sulfur when broken.

COLOR Pale yellow, but can become darker when weathered

HARDNESS 6.0–6.5

LUSTER Metallic

CLEAVAGE/FRACTURE Poor, breaks unevenly

SPECIFIC GRAVITY 4.95–5.10

STREAK Black-greenish to brownish black

HABIT Forms perfect cubes, but is often just found as a mass of pyrite or intergrown with other minerals

COMPOSITION FeS (Iron sulfide)

MINERAL GROUP Sulfides and friends

Pyrrhotite (pir-ho-tite)

Pyrrhotite is often called magnetic pyrite because it has a similar chemistry to pyrite but is weakly magnetic. It occurs in some igneous rocks like norites, in veins, and in some layered, cooled molten rocks, along with nickel minerals. If it is a mineral in rocks used to make concrete, it can react in a way that causes the concrete to crumble.

COLOR Bronze

HARDNESS 3.5–4.5

LUSTER Metallic

CLEAVAGE/FRACTURE None

SPECIFIC GRAVITY 4.6

STREAK Dark gray

HABIT Tabular crystals or massive

COMPOSITION FeS (Iron sulfide)

MINERAL GROUP Sulfides and friends

Gold (gold)

Gold is probably the most-desired mineral in the entire world. It is a native element. Other minerals are often mistaken for it, mostly because people have hopes that they can find it anywhere. Actually, the truth is that gold is rare. It is easy to identify as long as you do more than just look at color. It is *very* heavy (over 19 times as heavy as water) and *very* soft, and its streak is gold (never white or black). You can find gold in veins in rock, but mostly people find it by using a gold pan.

COLOR Gold

HARDNESS 2.5

LUSTER Metallic yellow

CLEAVAGE/FRACTURE None, easily beaten into a sheet

SPECIFIC GRAVITY 19.3

STREAK Gold

HABIT Normally found as nuggets, flakes, and grains in rivers, but sometimes as crystals in veins

COMPOSITION Au (Gold)

MINERAL GROUP Native elements

Copper (cop-per)

Copper can be found as a native element in a few places on the planet, but the largest deposits are in the upper peninsula of Michigan. This form of copper was mined by ancient people for tools and bowls.

COLOR Red, but is often tarnished to green on the outside

HARDNESS 2.5–3.0

LUSTER Metallic

CLEAVAGE/FRACTURE None

SPECIFIC GRAVITY 8.95

STREAK Copper red

HABIT Can grow into cube-shaped crystals, but most commonly found as flattened nuggets

COMPOSITION Cu (Copper)

MINERAL GROUP Native elements

Bismuth (bis–muth)

Bismuth can form in nature as a native element. However, most bismuth crystals seen at mineral shows are not naturally occurring—they are grown. The crystals are extremely pretty and show a strange hoppered pattern, which looks like a hollow step pyramid. Sometimes they display peacock feather colors.

COLOR Metallic blue to metallic silver

HARDNESS 2.0–2.5

LUSTER Metallic

CLEAVAGE/FRACTURE None

SPECIFIC GRAVITY 9.8

STREAK Silver gray

HABIT Hoppered crystals

COMPOSITION Bi (Bismuth)

MINERAL GROUP Native elements

Bornite (bor–nite)

See full fact sheet on page 87.

Feldspar (feld-spar)

Feldspar is a family of minerals that makes up around 40% of all the minerals in the Earth's crust, so you will probably be seeing a lot of it! It comes in many different varieties. The two major types are orthoclase and plagioclase. They form from the cooling of molten rock, so they are found in all igneous rocks. They can also be found in metamorphic rocks. In some special cases, they can be found in sedimentary rocks. Feldspar is used to make pottery and paint. Over time, it breaks down to form clay minerals. We find a lot of clay forming when rocks break down to soil.

COLOR White, pink, gray

HARDNESS 6-6.5

LUSTER Vitreous

CLEAVAGE/FRACTURE Good, in two or three directions, forming rhomb shapes and faces when broken

SPECIFIC GRAVITY 2.6

STREAK White

HABIT Tabular or rectangular crystals, sometimes twins

COMPOSITION $KAlSi_3O_8$ (Potassium aluminum silicate), $NaAlSi_3O_8$ (Albite), $CaAl_2Si_2O_8$ (Anorthite)

MINERAL GROUP Silicates: Framework structure

Mica (mi-ca)

Mica is a family of minerals that all have a very distinctive cleavage: they all form sheets like a book that you can easily pull apart into almost transparent pages. Because of this amazing feature, you will find them easy to identify. They come in many colors, with the most common being a silvery-white mica called muscovite and a dark black mica called biotite. Micas can be found in many igneous rocks. They also grow well in metamorphic rocks, like schists and gneiss, which are full of mica grains. Mica has been used as a substitute for glass, in electrical devices like toasters, and in many electronic parts.

COLOR Silver-white, black, yellow, pink, green

HARDNESS 2.5-4

LUSTER Pearly

CLEAVAGE/FRACTURE Perfect, along one direction to form sheets

SPECIFIC GRAVITY 2.9

STREAK White

HABIT Forms sheets

COMPOSITION $KAl_2(AlSi_3O_{10})(F,OH)_2$ (Potassium aluminum silicate)

MINERAL GROUP Silicates: Sheet structure

Gypsum (gyp-sum)

Gypsum is a soft mineral, listed as number 2 on the Mohs Scale of Hardness. It is found in sedimentary rocks that form from the evaporation of water. It is used for many things such as plaster, blackboard chalk, and drywall boards. It has some sister minerals—like alabaster and selenite. Over time, gypsum will dissolve back into water.

COLOR White, but can be stained pinkish to brown

HARDNESS 2

LUSTER Silky or pearly

CLEAVAGE/FRACTURE Good, in two directions

SPECIFIC GRAVITY 2.32

STREAK White

HABIT Forms elongated prisms, which can be twinned

COMPOSITION $CaSO_4 \cdot 2H_2O$ (Hydrated calcium sulfate)

MINERAL GROUP Carbonates and friends

Actinolite (ac-tyn-o-lite)

See full fact sheet on page 75.

Anorthoclase (an-or-tho-clase)

See full fact sheet on page 105.

Cerussite (ce-rus-site)

See full fact sheet on page 105.

Kaolinite (kay-o-lin-ite)

Kaolinite is a clay mineral that forms from the breaking down of other silicate minerals like feldspars, especially in places with hot and wet climates. It is often mined, and when that happens, it's called kaolin. Kaolinite is used for paint, cosmetics, and even toothpaste and to make paper glossy. It is one mineral that seems to have hundreds of uses!

COLOR White

HARDNESS 2.0–2.5

LUSTER Pearly to earthy

CLEAVAGE/FRACTURE
Perfect, in sheets, making it seem greasy

SPECIFIC GRAVITY 2.2–2.7

STREAK White

HABIT Mostly as massive clumps or layers, and very rarely as crystals

COMPOSITION $Al_2Si_2O_5(OH)_4$ (Hydrated aluminum silicate)

MINERAL GROUP Silicates: Sheet structure

Orthoclase (or-tho-clase)

See full fact sheet on page 86.

Talc (talc)

See full fact sheet on page 73.

Alabaster (al-a-bas-ter)

Alabaster is a soft mineral used to carve ornaments. It is a massive version of the mineral gypsum. It can also be a massive form of very fine-grained calcite and can also be called onyx. In ancient times, thin sheets of alabaster were used as small windows.

COLOR White, but can be stained pink, green, orange, or brown

HARDNESS 2–3

LUSTER Silky or pearly

CLEAVAGE/FRACTURE Good, in two directions

SPECIFIC GRAVITY 2.32

STREAK White

HABIT Massive

COMPOSITION $CaSO_3.2H_2O$ (Hydrated calcium sulfate)

MINERAL GROUP Carbonates and friends

Barite (bar-ite)

Barite is the main source of the element barium. Barite is used in paints, in glass, and for some medical purposes. It can be found in many types of ores and is often found with lead minerals.

COLOR White and clear

HARDNESS 3.0–3.5

LUSTER Vitreous or pearly

CLEAVAGE/FRACTURE Cleaves to form cubes

SPECIFIC GRAVITY 4.5–5.0

STREAK White

HABIT Can form tabular crystals or be fibrous

COMPOSITION $BaSO_4$ (Barium sulfate)

MINERAL GROUP Sulfides and friends

Dolomite (do-lo-mite)

Dolomite is a carbonate mineral not unlike calcite, except that it contains the element magnesium as well as calcium. It is common in older sedimentary rocks around the world. Dolomite has many uses, including as a fertilizer and a building stone.

COLOR White to gray

HARDNESS 3.5–4.0

LUSTER Vitreous and pearly

CLEAVAGE/FRACTURE
Cleaves in three directions, but not at right angles

SPECIFIC GRAVITY 2.85

STREAK White

HABIT Tabular crystals, granular, massive

COMPOSITION $CaMg(CO_3)_2$ (Calcium magnesium carbonate)

MINERAL GROUP
Carbonates and friends

Aragonite (a-ra-go-nite)

Aragonite is the sister mineral to calcite. It has the same chemistry, but it has a different crystal structure, which means it has different properties. It forms as part of animal shells and corals, which can make up limestone. Being a carbonate mineral, it easily reacts to acid.

COLOR White, but can be many colors due to impurities

HARDNESS 3.5–4.0

LUSTER Vitreous

CLEAVAGE/FRACTURE
Tends to break along surfaces

SPECIFIC GRAVITY 2.95

STREAK White

HABIT Forms many shapes, and crystals can be prisms

COMPOSITION $CaCO_3$ (Calcium carbonate)

MINERAL GROUP
Carbonates and friends

Wollastonite (wol-las-ton-ite)

Wollastonite is a mineral that forms when limestone is cooked during metamorphism. It is often found with other metamorphic minerals like garnets. It's an important mineral used to make ceramics, paint, and steel.

COLOR White

HARDNESS 4.5–5.0

LUSTER Vitreous

CLEAVAGE/FRACTURE Forms splinters

SPECIFIC GRAVITY 2.9

STREAK White

HABIT Forms radiating crystals, sometimes fibers

COMPOSITION $CaSiO_3$ (Calcium silicate)

MINERAL GROUP Silicates: Chain structure

Tremolite (trem-o-lite)

Tremolite is a mineral of the amphibole family of rock forming minerals. It forms in metamorphic rocks that are rich in dolomite and quartz. The mineral forms radiating crystals, but can also be fibrous. In that form, it is a type of asbestos that is dangerous and needs to be stored in a sealed jar.

COLOR White or green

HARDNESS 5–6

LUSTER Vitreous

CLEAVAGE/FRACTURE Perfect

SPECIFIC GRAVITY 3.0

STREAK White

HABIT Forms elongated, often radiating crystals, and can also be fibrous

COMPOSITION $Ca_2(Mg,Fe)Si_8O_{22}(OH)_2$ (Calcium magnesium and/or iron silicate)

MINERAL GROUP Silicates: Chain structure

Opal (o-pal)

Opal is a strange form of silica, which technically is not a mineral as its atoms are not in an ordered structure. It is often called a mineraloid. It forms in cracks in any form of rock at low temperatures and can replace wood and fossil shells. It comes in two forms: precious opal has flashes of color called iridescence, and common opal shows no color flashes. It is best when stored in water so that it does not dry out.

COLOR White, but can come in many colors, including black, which is the most sought-after

HARDNESS 5.5–6.0

LUSTER Waxy

CLEAVAGE/FRACTURE None, but breaks with rounded surfaces

SPECIFIC GRAVITY 2.15

STREAK White

HABIT Forms in cracks and veins, and can also be found as nodules and masses

COMPOSITION $SiO_2 \cdot H_2O$ (Hydrated silica)

MINERAL GROUP Silicates: No structure

Ulexite (u-lex-ite)

See full fact sheet on page 104.

Crocidolite (cro-sid-o-lite)

See full fact sheet on page 84.

Plagioclase (pla-gio-clase)

Plagioclase is a feldspar mineral found in gabbro and basalt. It actually is a group of minerals that have slightly different chemistry with changing amounts of sodium and calcium. When exposed to the weather, plagioclase breaks down over time to form clay.

COLOR White or gray

HARDNESS 6.0–6.5

LUSTER Vitreous

CLEAVAGE/FRACTURE Good, two directions that form almost a right angle

SPECIFIC GRAVITY 2.6–2.8

STREAK White

HABIT Long tabular crystals, but sometimes forms twins

COMPOSITION $NaAlSi_3O_8$ (Albite), $CaAl_2Si_2O_8$ (Anorthite)

MINERAL GROUP Silicates: Framework structure

Milky Quartz (mil-key kworts)

Milky quartz is a white variety of the mineral quartz. It is quite common to find milky quartz making up veins in other rocks. Sometimes they form white crystals in small vugs in the veins.

COLOR White

HARDNESS 7

LUSTER Vitreous

CLEAVAGE/FRACTURE No cleavage, breaks in curved surfaces

SPECIFIC GRAVITY 2.65

STREAK White

HABIT Six-sided prisms ending often in six-sided points

COMPOSITION SiO_2 (Silicon dioxide)

MINERAL GROUP Silicates: Framework structure

Sillimanite (sil–li–man–ite)

Sillimanite is a metamorphic mineral that occurs in rocks that have undergone a high level of cooking at any amount of pressure. It is commonly found in a metamorphic rock called gneiss. Sillimanite is part of a three-mineral family, along with andalusite and kyanite.

COLOR White, green, or colorless

HARDNESS 7

LUSTER Vitreous

CLEAVAGE/FRACTURE Good

SPECIFIC GRAVITY 3.24

STREAK White

HABIT Normally grows fibrous crystals

COMPOSITION Al_2SiO_5 (Aluminum silicate)

MINERAL GROUP Silicates: Single block structure

Beryl (behr–il)

Beryl is a mineral found in pegmatites within or near granite bodies. It can form very large six-sided crystals, and different colors form the gemstones aquamarine (blue) and emerald (green).

COLOR White or clear

HARDNESS 7.5–8.0

LUSTER Vitreous

CLEAVAGE/FRACTURE Forms some almost flat surfaces

SPECIFIC GRAVITY 2.76

STREAK White

HABIT Tabular or columnar crystals

COMPOSITION $Be_3Al_2Si_6O_{18}$ (Beryllium aluminum silicate)

MINERAL GROUP Silicates: Ring structure

Olivine (oliv-een)

Olivine is a green mineral that is common in the Earth's upper mantle. It can be brought up to the surface by volcanic eruptions. It is often found as larger crystals inside a fine-grained black volcanic rock. It can be found in basalt, a volcanic rock, and in gabbro, an igneous rock. When these rocks are molten, olivine is the very first mineral to start forming. Some special forms of basalt, called picrate, can contain large crystals of olivine. There is even a beach in Hawaii that is made of olivine, so the sand looks green! Gem-quality olivine is often sold under the name peridot.

COLOR Green and yellow-green

HARDNESS 6.5-7

LUSTER Vitreous

CLEAVAGE/FRACTURE Brittle, breaks with curved surfaces

SPECIFIC GRAVITY 3.2-4.5

STREAK White (but difficult to test as olivine is a hard mineral!)

HABIT Forms mineral grains

COMPOSITION (Mg, Fe)2SiO4 (Iron magnesium silicate)

MINERAL GROUP Silicates: Single block structure

Amphibole (am-fi-bol)

Amphiboles are a family of minerals that form prism or needle-like minerals. Amphibole can be found in igneous and metamorphic rocks. The most common is called hornblende; other common amphiboles are tremolite and actinolite. Many of the amphibole minerals are commonly called asbestos, which are usually brown or blue. If you collect any of those fibrous minerals you should store and display them in a closed jar so that you don't breathe in the small fibers.

COLOR Green, brown, black, white, yellow, blue

HARDNESS 5-6

LUSTER Vitreous to dull

CLEAVAGE/FRACTURE Good, in two directions, but not at right angles

SPECIFIC GRAVITY 3.0-3.4

STREAK White to gray

HABIT Tabular to fibrous

COMPOSITION $(K,Na)_{0-1}$ $(Ca,Na,Fe,Mg)_2(Mg,Fe,Al)_5(Al,Si)_8$ $O_{22}(OH)_2$ (Complex aluminum silicate)

MINERAL GROUP Silicates: Chain structure

Pyroxene (pi-rox-een)

Pyroxenes are a family of rock forming minerals that is found in igneous and metamorphic rocks. A common pyroxene mineral found in dark volcanic rocks is augite, but a more famous pyroxene is jade. Most of the pyroxenes are dark green or brown in color, and all have similar properties. The name pyroxene comes from the Greek phrase "fire stranger," as these minerals are often found in dark volcanic rocks along with olivine and amphiboles. They have even found a meteorite from Mars that is made of almost all pyroxene!

COLOR Dark green to brown, black.

HARDNESS 5-6

LUSTER Vitreous

CLEAVAGE/FRACTURE Good, almost right angles

SPECIFIC GRAVITY 3.2-3.5

STREAK White, greenish

HABIT Stubby crystals, square

COMPOSITION (NaCa) $(Mg,Fe,Al)(Al,Si)_2O_6$ (Sodium calcium magnesium iron aluminum silicate)

MINERAL GROUP Silicates: Chain structure

Talc (talc)

Talc is one of the softest minerals, and is number 1 on the Mohs Scale. In its massive form it is called soapstone. It has been used for thousands of years as a crushed-up powder for makeup and baby powder and even in paper and paint. It forms in metamorphic rock when mountains are being built.

COLOR Green or white

HARDNESS 1

LUSTER Waxy

CLEAVAGE/FRACTURE
Forms flat sheets, but is so soft it tends to powder

SPECIFIC GRAVITY 2.7

STREAK White

HABIT Massive, can look like it is in layers or even fibers

COMPOSITION $Mg_3Si_4O_{10}(OH)_2$ (Magnesium silicate)

MINERAL GROUP Silicates: Sheet structure

Cummingtonite (come-ing-ton-ite)

Cummingtonite is found in some metamorphic rocks, and it can have a range of chemistries. It belongs to the amphibole family of rock forming minerals. It can be found in a form that is fibrous, which makes it like one of the asbestos minerals.

COLOR Dark green

HARDNESS 5-6

LUSTER Silky

CLEAVAGE/FRACTURE
Good, in two directions

SPECIFIC GRAVITY 3.1-3.6

STREAK White

HABIT Fibrous or radiating crystals or long crystals

COMPOSITION
$(Mg,Fe)_7Si_8O_{22}(OH)_2$ (Hydrated magnesium/iron silicate)

MINERAL GROUP Silicates: Chain structure

Apatite (ap-a-tite)

Apatite is a small family of minerals that are often mistaken for other things. In fact, the name means "to deceive." The fluorine-rich apatite is used in toothpastes to provide fluoride to strengthen teeth. It is often also used to make fertilizer. The largest deposits of apatite are found in sedimentary rocks. Apatite is listed as number 5 on the Mohs Scale of Hardness.

COLOR Pale green or colorless

HARDNESS 5

LUSTER Vitreous

CLEAVAGE/FRACTURE Poor

SPECIFIC GRAVITY 3.16–3.22

STREAK White

HABIT Forms tabular crystals, but can be found in grains

COMPOSITION $Ca_5(PO_4)_3(F,Cl,OH)$ (Calcium phosphate with either fluorine, chlorine, or hydroxide molecules attached)

MINERAL GROUP Carbonates and friends

Sapphire (sa-fire)

See full fact sheet on page 82.

Tremolite (trem-o-lite)

See full fact sheet on page 66.

Actinolite (ac-tyn-o-lite)

Actinolite is a common metamorphic mineral found in rocks that are close to large granite molten rocks that have cooled. Actinolite forms blades or fibrous crystals. Some forms of actinolite are used as gemstones, known as jade.

COLOR Green, white, or black

HARDNESS 5–6

LUSTER Vitreous

CLEAVAGE/FRACTURE Cleaves along one surface, fractures unevenly

SPECIFIC GRAVITY 3.0

STREAK White

HABIT Bladed, fibrous, or radiating crystal clumps

COMPOSITION $Ca_2(Mg,Fe)Si_8O_{22}(OH)_2$ (Calcium iron/magnesium silicate)

MINERAL GROUP Silicates

Diopside (di-op-side)

Diopside is a mineral that belongs to the pyroxene family. It is found in some igneous rocks, some basalts, and some metamorphic rocks. Diopside is used to make gemstones called a Siberian emerald and a black star diopside.

COLOR Green

HARDNESS 5.5–6.5

LUSTER Vitreous

CLEAVAGE/FRACTURE One direction, fractures with curved surfaces

SPECIFIC GRAVITY 3.3

STREAK White

HABIT Short prism-shaped crystals

COMPOSITION $MgCaSi_2O_6$ (Magnesium calcium silicate)

MINERAL GROUP Silicates: Chain structure

Nephrite (nef-rite)

Nephrite is one of the gem minerals commonly called jade. The other is jadeite. Nephrite belongs to the family of amphiboles. It is formed in metamorphic rocks that have undergone very high pressures and low temperatures. It takes an expert to tell it apart from jadeite.

COLOR Green, but can also be yellow to brown

HARDNESS 6.0–6.5

LUSTER Vitreous to pearly

CLEAVAGE/FRACTURE Splinters when fractured

SPECIFIC GRAVITY 2.95

STREAK White

HABIT Mostly massive

COMPOSITION $Ca_2(Mg,Fe)_5Si_8O_{22}(OH)_2$ (Calcium magnesium/iron silicate)

MINERAL GROUP Silicates: Chain structure

Amazonite (am-a-zon-ite)

Amazonite belongs to the feldspar family of minerals. It has been used as a gemstone for thousands of years—it has even been found in the tombs of Egyptian royalty. It is located in many states in the USA. It tends not to keep its shine when polished.

COLOR Green

HARDNESS 6.0–6.5

LUSTER Vitreous

CLEAVAGE/FRACTURE Good, breaks into rhombohedrons

SPECIFIC GRAVITY 2.58

STREAK White

HABIT Forms prisms

COMPOSITION $KAlSi_3O_8$ (Potassium aluminum silicate)

MINERAL GROUP Silicates: Framework structure

Jadeite (jade-ite)

Jadeite is one of the gem minerals commonly called jade. The other is nephrite. Jadeite belongs to the mineral family of pyroxenes. It is formed in metamorphic rocks that have undergone both very high pressures and low temperatures. It takes an expert to tell it apart from nephrite.

COLOR Green

HARDNESS 6.5–7.0

LUSTER Vitreous or pearly

CLEAVAGE/FRACTURE
Splinters when fractured

SPECIFIC GRAVITY
3.24–3.43

STREAK White

HABIT Mostly massive

COMPOSITION $NaAlSi_2O_6$
(Sodium aluminum silicate)

MINERAL GROUP Silicates:
Chain structure

Emerald (em-er-ald)

Emerald is the green gemstone form of the mineral beryl. The green color comes from impurities of the elements chromium or vanadium. They often have many small inclusions that make the emerald fragile.

COLOR Green

HARDNESS 7.5–8.0

LUSTER Vitreous

CLEAVAGE/FRACTURE
Forms some almost flat surfaces

SPECIFIC GRAVITY 2.76

STREAK White

HABIT Tabular or columnar crystals

COMPOSITION $Be3Al_2Si_6O_{18}$
(Beryllium aluminum silicate)

MINERAL GROUP Silicates:
Ring structure

Epidote (ep-i-dote)

Epidote is a common rock forming mineral that can be found in igneous rocks like basalt. As a collectable mineral, it is mostly found in metamorphic rocks, like marble and hornfels. It can also be found in pegmatites. Epidote is often the highlight of some people's collections due to its delicate crystals.

COLOR Green to yellow-green

HARDNESS 6–7

LUSTER Vitreous

CLEAVAGE/FRACTURE Perfect, in one direction, and good, in a second

SPECIFIC GRAVITY 3.3–3.6

STREAK Gray

HABIT Forms elongated, intergrown crystals, but also found as massive clumps

COMPOSITION $Ca_2(Al,Fe)_2(SiO_4)_3(OH)$ (Calcium-rich aluminum silicate)

MINERAL GROUP Silicates: Double block structure

Titanite (ti-ta-nite)

See full fact sheet on page 114.

Chlorite (klo-rite)

Chlorite is a mica-like mineral that forms from other minerals due to metamorphism or other alteration. It is common in some ore deposits that have been formed by very hot water. Sometimes chlorite can be found as small fragments inside other minerals, like quartz.

COLOR Green

HARDNESS 2.0–2.5

LUSTER Vitreous

CLEAVAGE/FRACTURE
Perfect, forms sheets

SPECIFIC GRAVITY 2.6–3.3

STREAK Pale green

HABIT Flaky

COMPOSITION $(Mg,Fe)_3(Si,Al)_4O_{10}(OH)_2.(Mg,Fe)_3(OH)_6$ (Magnesium/iron silicate)

MINERAL GROUP Silicates: Sheet structure

Malachite (mal-a-kite)

Malachite is a green copper mineral and often forms rounded masses that have banding. It can also form a staining on the outside of other copper minerals. It is often found with the blue copper mineral azurite.

COLOR Green

HARDNESS 7.5

LUSTER Vitreous, but can be dull or earthy

CLEAVAGE/FRACTURE
Good, along one surface, but fractures unevenly

SPECIFIC GRAVITY 3.6

STREAK Light green

HABIT Mostly massive or as a coating

COMPOSITION $Cu_2CO_3(OH)_2$ (Copper carbonate with water)

MINERAL GROUP
Carbonates and friends

Turquoise (tur-quoiz)

See full fact sheet on page 84.

Kyanite (ky-a-nite)

Kyanite is a metamorphic mineral that occurs in rocks that have undergone a low level of cooking and up to very high amounts of pressure. It is commonly found in the metamorphic rock types gneiss and schist, and it can also be found in pegmatites. It is part of a three-mineral family, along with andalusite and sillimanite, which can tell us about the grade of metamorphism of the rock.

COLOR Blue

HARDNESS 4.5 in one direction, and 7 in the other direction

LUSTER Vitreous

CLEAVAGE/FRACTURE Good, fractures in splinters

SPECIFIC GRAVITY 3.6

STREAK White

HABIT Normally grows in blades

COMPOSITION Al_2SiO_5 (Aluminum silicate)

MINERAL GROUP Silicates: Single block structure

Sodalite (so–da–lite)

Sodalite is a mineral often used to make ornaments and jewelry. It is found in veins in some igneous rocks. If placed under an ultraviolet light, it will shine with a bright orange glow. It is sometimes mistaken for lapis lazuli, another blue mineral.

COLOR Blue, royal blue

HARDNESS 5.5–6.0

LUSTER Dull or vitreous

CLEAVAGE/FRACTURE Poor

SPECIFIC GRAVITY 2.2–2.3

STREAK White

HABIT Massive clumps

COMPOSITION
$Na_8(Al_6Si_6O_{24})Cl_2$ (Complex aluminum silicate)

MINERAL GROUP Silicates: Framework structure

Labradorite (lab–ra–dor–ite)

Labradorite is a feldspar mineral often seen in countertops as an iridescent blue mineral. It is a spectacular display mineral that changes colors as it moves in the light. In fact, it's so spectacular that it is made into jewelry.

COLOR Blue to green

HARDNESS 6.0–6.5

LUSTER Vitreous or pearly

CLEAVAGE/FRACTURE
Perfect in one direction, at right angles in another

SPECIFIC GRAVITY 2.7

STREAK White

HABIT Crystals are thin, can twin, or striated with small grooves

COMPOSITION
$(Ca,Na)(Al,Si)_4O_8$ (Calcium/sodium aluminum silicate)

MINERAL GROUP Silicates: Framework structure

Aquamarine (a-qua-ma-rine)

Aquamarine is the blue gemstone form of the mineral beryl. The blue color comes from impurities in the element iron. Aquamarine is often found with white beryl crystals.

COLOR Blue

HARDNESS 7.5–8.0

LUSTER Vitreous

CLEAVAGE/FRACTURE
Forms some almost flat surfaces

SPECIFIC GRAVITY 2.76

STREAK White

HABIT Tabular or columnar crystals

COMPOSITION $Be_3Al_2Si_6O_{18}$ (Beryllium aluminum silicate)

MINERAL GROUP Silicates: Ring structure

Sapphire (sa-fire)

Sapphire is a gem variety of the mineral corundum. It is the most precious and valuable blue gemstone, but it can come in other colors as well. It is a pleochroic mineral, which means that it can be a slightly different color when viewed from different directions.

COLOR Blue, green, or yellow

HARDNESS 9

LUSTER Vitreous

CLEAVAGE/FRACTURE
None

SPECIFIC GRAVITY 4.0

STREAK White, but impossible to test because it is so hard

HABIT Forms six-sided crystals

COMPOSITION Al_2O_3 (Aluminum oxide)

MINERAL GROUP Oxides and friends

Covellite (co-ve-lite)

Covellite is a copper mineral found as a coating or as a minor mineral in copper deposits. It is not a copper ore mineral. Recently, it was discovered that covellite is a super conductor, and it is being researched for use in batteries.

COLOR Blue

HARDNESS 1.3–2.0

LUSTER Almost metallic

CLEAVAGE/FRACTURE
Perfect, in one direction

SPECIFIC GRAVITY 4.7

STREAK Gray

HABIT Thin, platy crystals, or coatings on other copper minerals

COMPOSITION CuS
(Copper sulfide)

MINERAL GROUP Sulfides and friends

Azurite (a-zur-ite)

Azurite is a dark blue copper mineral. It is often formed by the weathering of other copper minerals and can stain the outside of copper-bearing rocks. It is often found with the green mineral malachite.

COLOR Dark blue

HARDNESS 3.5–4

LUSTER Vitreous

CLEAVAGE/FRACTURE
Cleaves along one surface, and fractures like glass

SPECIFIC GRAVITY 3.7

STREAK Light blue

HABIT Mostly massive, can form prism-shaped crystals

COMPOSITION
$Cu_3(CO_3)_2(OH)_2$ (Copper carbonate hydrated with water)

MINERAL GROUP
Carbonates and friends

Turquoise (tur-quoiz)

Turquoise is a mineral that forms from the alteration and weathering of copper and aluminum-rich minerals. It has a unique color between blue and green, and because of its color, since ancient times, turquoise has been prized as a gemstone.

COLOR Blue-green

HARDNESS 5–6

LUSTER Waxy

CLEAVAGE/FRACTURE Normally not seen

SPECIFIC GRAVITY 2.6–2.9

STREAK Bluish white

HABIT Massive, nodules and coatings on other minerals

COMPOSITION
$CuAl_6(PO_4)_4(OH)_8 \cdot 4H_2O$
(Hydrated copper phosphate)

MINERAL GROUP
Carbonates and friends

Crocidolite (cro-sid-o-lite)

Crocidolite is often called blue asbestos and is thought to be the most dangerous of the asbestos minerals. It has caused lung diseases in people who live and/or work with it. It is actually a fibrous form of the mineral riebeckite.

COLOR Blue or black

HARDNESS 6

LUSTER Vitreous or like silk

CLEAVAGE/FRACTURE Forms long fibers of mineral

SPECIFIC GRAVITY 3.4

STREAK Pale blue

HABIT Fibers, but can form prism-shaped crystals

COMPOSITION $Na_2(Fe^{2+}_3Fe^{3+}_2)Si_8O_{22}(OH)_2$ (Sodium-rich amphibole silicate)

MINERAL GROUP Silicates: Chain structure

Rhodochrosite (ro-do-crow-site)

Rhodochrosite is one of the prettiest minerals. It is an ore of the metal manganese that forms in veins. Because it is soft, it is not made into gems, but is often used in jewelry. It can still be found in the waste dumps of old silver mines.

COLOR Deep pink to red

HARDNESS 3.5–4.0

LUSTER Vitreous

CLEAVAGE/FRACTURE Perfect

SPECIFIC GRAVITY 3.7

STREAK White

HABIT Rhombohedron-shaped crystals, bladed, columns, or massive

COMPOSITION $MnCO_3$ (Manganese carbonate)

MINERAL GROUP Carbonates and friends

Rose Quartz (rose kworts)

Rose quartz is a pink variety of quartz. Impurities within the quartz give it its pink color.

COLOR Pink

HARDNESS 7

LUSTER Vitreous

CLEAVAGE/FRACTURE None, breaks in curved surfaces

SPECIFIC GRAVITY 2.65

STREAK White

HABIT Six-sided prisms ending often in six-sided points

COMPOSITION SiO_2 (Silicon dioxide)

MINERAL GROUP Silicates: Framework structure

Orthoclase (or–tho–clase)

Orthoclase is a feldspar mineral found in granites. It can sometimes make up almost half of the minerals in the rock. In some places, it can form large pink crystals in the granite. It is listed as number 6 on the Mohs Scale of Hardness, and although it is harder than glass, when ground up, orthoclase is often used for making some glasses, as well as pottery glazes. When exposed to the weather, it breaks down over time to form clay. It is often called K-spar, because it contains potassium, which has as its chemical symbol K.

COLOR Pink or white

HARDNESS 6

LUSTER Vitreous, pearly

CLEAVAGE/FRACTURE
Good, two directions that form a right angle where they meet

SPECIFIC GRAVITY 2.6

STREAK White

HABIT Long, tabular crystals, sometimes forms twins

COMPOSITION $KAlSi_3O_8$ (Potassium aluminum silicate)

MINERAL GROUP Silicates: Framework structure

Amethyst (am–e–thist)

Amethyst is the violet variety of quartz. It is often found in clusters of crystals and geodes. Amethyst is the official state gemstone of South Carolina.

COLOR Violet to purple

HARDNESS 7

LUSTER Vitreous

CLEAVAGE/FRACTURE None, breaks in curved surfaces

SPECIFIC GRAVITY 2.65

STREAK White

HABIT Six-sided prisms ending often in six-sided points

COMPOSITION SiO_2 (Silicon dioxide)

MINERAL GROUP Silicates: Framework structure

Bornite (bor–nite)

Bornite is a copper ore mineral that is copper red when fresh, but tarnishes to show bright blues and purples. It is often called "peacock ore" because it has the same colors as a peacock's tail.

COLOR Blue and purple with copper red when fresh

HARDNESS 3.0–3.5

LUSTER Metallic

CLEAVAGE/FRACTURE Poor, breaks unevenly

SPECIFIC GRAVITY 5

STREAK Grayish black

HABIT Mostly massive

COMPOSITION Cu_5FeS_4 (Copper iron sulfide)

MINERAL GROUP Sulfides and friends

Citrine (ci–trine)

Citrine is a yellow variety of the mineral quartz. Sometimes it is called the "money stone," because in ancient times people believed that citrine could bring you wealth.

COLOR Yellow to brown

HARDNESS 7

LUSTER Vitreous

CLEAVAGE/FRACTURE None, breaks in curved surfaces

SPECIFIC GRAVITY 2.65

STREAK White

HABIT Six-sided prisms ending often in six-sided points

COMPOSITION SiO_2 (Silicon dioxide)

MINERAL GROUP Silicates: Framework structure

Amber (am–ber)

Amber is fossilized tree resin, so *technically*, it's not a mineral. But so many people have amber in their collections that it has become a common treasure to hunt for and collect. It often contains other materials that were trapped in its very soft, sticky resin, including insects!

COLOR Yellow

HARDNESS 1–3

LUSTER Like resin

CLEAVAGE/FRACTURE None, but can break with round surfaces

SPECIFIC GRAVITY 1.0

STREAK White

HABIT Normally found in clumps, and can be water worn into rounded pebbles

COMPOSITION Organic tree resins, and the chemistry can vary based on the original tree

MINERAL GROUP None

Siderite (sid-er-ite)

Siderite is an iron ore mineral that can form in sedimentary rocks such as sandstone and shale. Sometimes, siderite is found as a concentrated, hard, solid ball or shape inside layers of coal, and these can contain fossils. It can also be found in veins with other ore minerals like galena and barite.

COLOR Yellow to brown

HARDNESS 3.75–4.25

LUSTER Vitreous

CLEAVAGE/FRACTURE
Great in one direction, uneven fracture in other directions

SPECIFIC GRAVITY 3.96

STREAK White

HABIT Tabular crystals, but mostly massive

COMPOSITION $FeCO_3$ (Iron carbonate)

MINERAL GROUP
Carbonates and friends

Zircon (zir-con)

See full fact sheet on page 115.

Topaz (to-paz)

Topaz is found in silica-rich igneous rocks like granite and rhyolite, and it is common in pegmatites associated with those rocks. It is listed as number 8 on the Mohs Scale of Hardness and is the hardest of all the silicate minerals. Topaz is used as a gemstone, especially in its yellow and blue varieties. It is the state gemstone of Texas.

COLOR Yellow, brown, or blue

HARDNESS 8

LUSTER Vitreous

CLEAVAGE/FRACTURE Perfect, in one direction

SPECIFIC GRAVITY 3.5

STREAK White, but hard to identify because of its hardness

HABIT Crystals form prisms

COMPOSITION $Al_2SiO_4(F,OH)_2$ (Aluminum fluorine-rich silicate)

MINERAL GROUP Silicates: Single block structure

Diamond (di-a-mond)

Diamonds are one of the hardest minerals and are listed as number 10 on the Mohs Scale of Hardness. They are formed deep in the Earth and are brought to the surface in unique igneous rocks called kimberlites or lamproites. Diamonds are made of only the element carbon. If small amounts of other elements are introduced, they can change a diamond's color. You can search for diamonds yourself in Crater of Diamonds State Park in Arkansas!

COLOR Pale yellow, but can also be colorless, brown, gray, blue, orange, red, or pink

HARDNESS 10

LUSTER Diamond-like

CLEAVAGE/FRACTURE Perfectly, in four directions, and can also fracture with curved surfaces

SPECIFIC GRAVITY 3.5

STREAK Colorless, because a diamond is so hard it is almost impossible to get a streak

HABIT Eight-sided crystals

COMPOSITION C (Carbon)

MINERAL GROUP Native element

Sulfur (sul-fer)

This bright yellow native element is often found forming around the gas vents of volcanoes. It can also be found as coatings when other minerals containing sulfur break down due to weather.

COLOR Yellow

HARDNESS 1.5–2.5

LUSTER Greasy when a crystal, can be dull when a coating

CLEAVAGE/FRACTURE None

SPECIFIC GRAVITY 2.0

STREAK Yellow

HABIT Crystals can form blades and needles, while coatings are more like a powder

COMPOSITION S (Sulfur)

MINERAL GROUP Native elements

Sphalerite (sfal-er-ite)

See full fact sheet on page 112.

Biotite (Bi-o-tite)

Biotite is a very common rock forming mica. It is easy to identify, even when it occurs as small crystals in an igneous rock, such as granite, or a metamorphic rock like schist. It is also one of the fool's gold minerals that appear to look like small golden flakes in a gold pan. A quick look with a magnifying glass will let you know what you've found!

COLOR Black to brown

HARDNESS 2.3–3.0

LUSTER Vitreous

CLEAVAGE/FRACTURE Perfect, forms sheets that can be easily separated

SPECIFIC GRAVITY 2.7–3.3

STREAK White

HABIT Forms thin, flaky sheets

COMPOSITION $K(Mg,Fe)_3(AlSi_3O_{10})(F,OH)_2$ (Complex silicate minerals)

MINERAL GROUP Silicates: Sheet structure

Cassiterite (cas-sit-er-ite)

See full fact sheet on page 110.

Tourmaline (tour–ma–line)

Tourmaline is found in igneous rocks, and especially in holes and cavities that have large crystals. It can also be found in pegmatites around granite bodies. It can also form in some metamorphic rocks like gneiss. Tourmaline is the state mineral of Maine.

COLOR Black, rarely as other colors, and sometimes as more than one color, such as green and pink in "watermelon" varieties

HARDNESS 7.0–7.5

LUSTER Vitreous

CLEAVAGE/FRACTURE None, brittle

SPECIFIC GRAVITY 3.06

STREAK White

HABIT Long, thin crystals

COMPOSITION (Ca,K,Na) $(Al,Fe,Li,Mg,Mn)_3(Al,Cr,Fe,V)_6$ $(BO_3)_3(Si,Al,B)_6O_{18}(OH,F)_4$ (Very complex silicate)

MINERAL GROUP Silicates: Ring structure

Mica

See full fact sheet on page 61.

Pyroxene

See full fact sheet on page 72.

Augite (au-gite)

Augite is a common rock forming mineral that belongs to the pyroxene family of minerals. It is a major mineral in rocks like gabbro and basalt. It can also be found in metamorphic rocks that have been cooked up to high temperatures.

COLOR Black, brown, or green

HARDNESS 5.5–6.0

LUSTER Vitreous

CLEAVAGE/FRACTURE Good

SPECIFIC GRAVITY 3.2–3.6

STREAK Greenish white

HABIT Stubby, prism-shaped crystals

COMPOSITION $(Ca,Na)(Mg,Fe,Al,Ti)(Si,Al)_2O_6$ (Complex aluminum silicate)

MINERAL GROUP Silicates: Chain structure

Hornblende (horn-blend)

Hornblende is a common mineral that belongs to the amphibole group of common rock forming minerals. It can be found in most igneous rocks and some metamorphic rocks. It is the main mineral in the rock type called amphibolite.

COLOR Black to dark green

HARDNESS 5–6

LUSTER Vitreous

CLEAVAGE/FRACTURE Can cleave to form flat faces

SPECIFIC GRAVITY 2.9

STREAK Gray white

HABIT Six-sided crystals

COMPOSITION $Ca_2(Mg,Fe,Al)_5(Al,Si)_8O_{22}(OH)_2$ (Complex calcium aluminum silicate)

MINERAL GROUP Silicates: Chain structure

Jet (jet)

Jet is a semiprecious gemstone that is actually a form of coal; it is wood that has turned to stone. Technically, it is not a mineral at all, but a rock type that belongs in the coal group. However, it is often sold as a mineral at rock shows.

COLOR Black

HARDNESS 2.5–4.0

LUSTER Dull, but can take a shine

CLEAVAGE/FRACTURE Uneven

SPECIFIC GRAVITY 1.30–1.34

STREAK Brown

HABIT Found in layers

COMPOSITION C (Carbon)

MINERAL GROUP Coal macerals

Chromite (kro-mite)

Chromite is a group of minerals mined for the element chromium. They form in coarse-grained, very dark, mafic, igneous rocks. Used to make stainless steel, it is found in Montana, US, and in South Africa.

COLOR Black

HARDNESS 5.5

LUSTER Almost metallic

CLEAVAGE/FRACTURE Breaks unevenly and is brittle

SPECIFIC GRAVITY 4.5–4.8

STREAK Brown

HABIT Massive clumps

COMPOSITION $(Fe,Mg)Cr_2O_4$ (Iron/magnesium chromium oxide)

MINERAL GROUP Oxides and friends

Graphite (graf-ite)

Graphite is a mineral form of the element carbon. It forms at low temperatures and pressures, unlike the other carbon mineral that forms at high temperature and pressure—diamond! Graphite is used in pencil leads. It is found in metamorphic rocks, some igneous rocks, and meteorites, too!

COLOR Black to steel gray

HARDNESS 1–2

LUSTER Metallic

CLEAVAGE/FRACTURE Cleaves in one direction, breaks in flakes

SPECIFIC GRAVITY 1.9–2.3

STREAK Black

HABIT Six-sided groups of fine crystals, massive

COMPOSITION C (Carbon)

MINERAL GROUP Native elements

Ilmenite (ill-men-ite)

Ilmenite is a weak magnetic mineral found in metamorphic and igneous rocks. It is an important ore of titanium that is used for sunscreens, food, cosmetics, and more. It has even been found in moon rocks!

COLOR Black

HARDNESS 5–6

LUSTER Metallic

CLEAVAGE/FRACTURE None, breaks with curved surfaces

SPECIFIC GRAVITY 4.75

STREAK Black

HABIT Grains or massive

COMPOSITION $FeTiO_3$ (Iron titanium oxide)

MINERAL GROUP Oxides and friends

Magnetite (mag-ne-tite)

Magnetite is magnetic! It is a major ore mineral for iron. Ancient people called it lodestone and used it to make compass needles. It is found in almost all igneous and metamorphic rocks as small crystals.

COLOR Black

HARDNESS 5.5–6.5

LUSTER Metallic

CLEAVAGE/FRACTURE Poor, breaks unevenly

SPECIFIC GRAVITY 5.18

STREAK Black

HABIT Mostly massive, but can form eight-sided crystals

COMPOSITION Fe_2O_4 (Iron oxide)

MINERAL GROUP Oxides and friends

Pyrolusite (py-ro-lu-site)

Pyrolusite is an ore of the metal manganese. It forms around the famous "black smoker" hydrothermal vents found on parts of the ocean floor. In ancient times, it was crushed and used as a paint. It is still used today to color glass and bricks.

COLOR Black

HARDNESS 6.0–6.5, but can be as soft as 2

LUSTER Mostly dull, earthy

CLEAVAGE/FRACTURE Well, on one surface

SPECIFIC GRAVITY 4.4–5.0

STREAK Black and even bluish black

HABIT Mostly a massive mineral, powdery at times

COMPOSITION MnO_2 (Manganese oxide)

MINERAL GROUP Oxides and friends

Hematite (he-ma-tite)

Hematite is a common mineral found in all kinds of rocks and in soil. It is the major ore for iron. Unlike magnetite, the other major iron ore mineral, hematite is *not* magnetic. The largest deposits of hematite formed when the iron in the oceans all precipitated out because of the evolution of ocean plankton that produced oxygen.

COLOR Black to brown

HARDNESS 5.0–6.5

LUSTER Mostly earthy, but can be metallic

CLEAVAGE/FRACTURE None

SPECIFIC GRAVITY 5.0–5.3

STREAK Red to reddish brown

HABIT Massive, but can be thick crystals, be granular, and even form roselike features

COMPOSITION Fe_2O_3 (Iron oxide)

MINERAL GROUP Oxides and friends

Rutile (ru-tile)

See full fact sheet on page 113.

Quartz (kworts)

Quartz is the second most common mineral found on the surface of the Earth. It is found in igneous, sedimentary, and metamorphic rocks, and does not break down into other minerals. Sometimes you can find large white quartz veins cutting through rock layers that can be seen sticking out of fields. Quartz comes in many varieties, which are often given other names. For example, purple quartz is called amethyst. Pure quartz sand is often used to make glass. Quartz can form some beautiful hexagonal shaped long crystals. A very clear quartz crystal can be called Herkimer Diamond.

COLOR Colorless (most common), but also white, purple, pink, brown, red, and green

HARDNESS 7

LUSTER Glassy or vitreous; sometimes waxy or dull

CLEAVAGE/FRACTURE Breaks in rounded shapes

SPECIFIC GRAVITY 2.65

STREAK White

HABIT Six-sided prisms of crystals with a six-sided pyramid end, or massive with no crystals

COMPOSITION SiO_4 (Silicon oxide)

MINERAL GROUP Silicates: Framework structure

Calcite (cal-cite)

Calcite is a carbonate mineral found in sedimentary rocks like limestone as well as metamorphic (like marble) and even some rare igneous rocks. It can form beautiful rhomb-shaped prisms when broken. Its clearest form is often called "Iceland Spar," and when you place those rhombs over writing on paper, the writing looks like it is doubled. Calcite is also the mineral that makes up limestone caves. It is easily dissolved in rainwater and then recrystallized in caverns as stalagmites and stalactites. Calcite is often identified because it will react with acid and fizz.

COLOR Clear to white

HARDNESS 3 (it is on Mohs Scale of Hardness)

LUSTER Vitreous to pearly

CLEAVAGE/FRACTURE Perfect in three directions so it forms rhombs.

SPECIFIC GRAVITY 2.71

STREAK White

HABIT Crystalline, stalactite (like in caves), massive, and more

COMPOSITION $CaCO_3$ (Calcium carbonate)

MINERAL GROUP Carbonates and friends

Selenite (sel-e-nite)

Selenite is a sister mineral to gypsum. It often forms a crystal clump that looks like a rose and is sometimes called a "desert rose." This mineral does not contain the element selenite, although they have the same name. The name comes from the ancient Greek word for the sun.

COLOR Colorless to white

HARDNESS 2

LUSTER Silky or pearly

CLEAVAGE/FRACTURE Good, in two directions

SPECIFIC GRAVITY 2.32

STREAK White

HABIT Forms elongated crystal masses, and often grows in round clumps that look like flowers called roses

COMPOSITION $CaSO_4.2H_2O$ (Hydrated calcium sulfate)

MINERAL GROUP Carbonates and friends

Apatite (ap-a-tite)

See full fact sheet on page 74.

Diamond (di-a-mond)

See full fact sheet on page 91.

Sillimanite (sil-li-man-ite)

See full fact sheet on page 69.

Muscovite (mus-co-vite)

Muscovite is a very common mineral that belongs to the mica minerals. It can be found in igneous rocks like granite, as well as metamorphic rocks like schist. It is very common in pegmatites where you can find "books" of muscovite that are the size of quarters or larger.

COLOR Clear to silver

HARDNESS 2.0–2.5

LUSTER Vitreous, but can look metallic

CLEAVAGE/FRACTURE Perfect, forms mineral sheets

SPECIFIC GRAVITY 2.7–3.0

STREAK White

HABIT Forms books of platy minerals, can be six-sided

COMPOSITION $KAl_2(AlSi_3O_{10})(F,OH)_2$ (Potassium aluminum silicate)

MINERAL GROUP Silicates: Sheet structure

Herkimer Diamond (her-ki-mer di-a-mond)

Herkimer diamonds are very clear quartz crystals that form points at both ends. They are found in Herkimer County in New York State.

COLOR Clear

HARDNESS 7

LUSTER Vitreous

CLEAVAGE/FRACTURE None, breaks in curved surfaces

SPECIFIC GRAVITY 2.65

STREAK White

HABIT Six-sided prisms

COMPOSITION SiO_2 (Silicon oxide)

MINERAL GROUP Silicates: Framework structure

Halite (hay-lite)

Halite is rock salt—the same salt you sprinkle on food! It is formed when ocean water dries up, leaving behind a layer of salt crystals. Some halite is from when an ancient ocean dried up. Other halite has been formed by humans.

COLOR Clear, but can be stained by other things to be white or pink

HARDNESS 2.0–2.5

LUSTER Vitreous

CLEAVAGE/FRACTURE Forms cubes when broken

SPECIFIC GRAVITY 2.2

STREAK White

HABIT Cubes, massive

COMPOSITION NaCl (Sodium chloride)

MINERAL GROUP Oxides and friends

Ulexite (u-lex-ite)

Ulexite is sometimes called TV stone. It is made up of crystal fibers that conduct light along their thin shapes, just like fiber optic cables do in some televisions. It is found in rocks that formed from the evaporation of water.

COLOR Colorless to white

HARDNESS 2.5

LUSTER Vitreous

CLEAVAGE/FRACTURE Perfect, forms fibers

SPECIFIC GRAVITY 1.95

STREAK White

HABIT Fibrous

COMPOSITION
$NaCaB_5O_6(OH)_6 \cdot 5H_2O$ (Complex sodium borate hydroxide)

MINERAL GROUP Oxides and friends

Cerussite (ce-rus-site)

Cerussite is sometimes called white lead ore. Its clear form is called lead spar. It is an important ore of lead. Because of the way it twins, it forms very complex shapes as crystals, including stars, snowflakes, and large V's.

COLOR Clear to white

HARDNESS 3.0–3.5

LUSTER Diamond-like to vitreous

CLEAVAGE/FRACTURE Good, in two directions

SPECIFIC GRAVITY 6.5

STREAK White

HABIT Complex crystals, but can be massive

COMPOSITION $PbCO_3$ (Lead carbonate)

MINERAL GROUP Carbonates and friends

Anorthoclase (an-or-tho-clase)

Anorthoclase is a member of the family of feldspar. It is found in volcanic and coarse-grained igneous rocks that are very rich in sodium. It is strange in that its crystals can grow in two different shapes while its other properties remain the same.

COLOR Clear or white

HARDNESS 6

LUSTER Vitreous

CLEAVAGE/FRACTURE Forms flat crystal surfaces

SPECIFIC GRAVITY 2.57–2.60

STREAK White

HABIT Short prism-shaped crystals that can twin

COMPOSITION $(Na,K)AlSi_3O_8$ (Sodium-rich aluminum silicate)

MINERAL GROUP Silicates: Framework structure

Fluorite (fluo-rite)

Fluorite is a common mineral that is found in veins in granite, in metal deposits, and even in sedimentary limestone. It is used as a chemical to help melt metals, in ceramics, and sometimes to create a strong acid. Many fluorite crystals glow under ultraviolet light. This is a phenomenon called fluorescence, named after the mineral. Fluorite is listed as number 4 on the Mohs Scale of Hardness.

COLOR Clear, when pure, but can be almost any other color

HARDNESS 4

LUSTER Vitreous

CLEAVAGE/FRACTURE Perfect in one direction, good in another, and when broken, forms eight-sided crystals

SPECIFIC GRAVITY 3.1

STREAK White

HABIT Forms a mix of cubes, and eight-sided and twelve-sided crystals

COMPOSITION CaF_2 (Calcium fluoride)

MINERAL GROUP Oxides and friends

Alabaster (al-a-bas-ter)

See full fact sheet on page 64.

Gypsum (gyp-sum)

See full fact sheet on page 62.

Tiger's Eye (ti-gers eye)

Tiger's eye, or just tiger eye, is actually the growth of two minerals together. The first is a form of the mineral quartz, which is grown into a type of amphibole mineral. The result is a banded mineral that looks like the colors of a cat's eye. The color comes from small grains of iron ore in the structure, so this is quite a complex mineral form! It is seen a lot at mineral shows and is made into jewelry.

COLOR Browns and yellows

HARDNESS 5.5–6.0

LUSTER Silky

CLEAVAGE/FRACTURE None

SPECIFIC GRAVITY 2.6–2.7

STREAK White

HABIT Massive, in bands

COMPOSITION SiO_2 (Silicon dioxide)

MINERAL GROUP Silicates: No structure

Barite (bar-ite)

See full fact sheet on page 64.

Siderite (sid-er-ite)

See full fact sheet on page 89.

Agate (ag-at)

Technically, agate is a rock and not a mineral. It is made up of layers of different-colored chalcedony, which is a variety of quartz. However, agate is often grouped with minerals in collections. It is used for many types of jewelry and ornaments, including bowls and lamps.

COLOR Brown with bandings of red, white, or yellow

HARDNESS 6.5–7.0

LUSTER Waxy

CLEAVAGE/FRACTURE Fractures with curved surfaces

SPECIFIC GRAVITY 2.58–2.64

STREAK White

HABIT Massive

COMPOSITION SiO_2 (Silicon dioxide)

MINERAL GROUP Silicates: Framework structure

Andalusite (an-da-lu-site)

Andalusite is a metamorphic mineral that occurs in rocks that have undergone a medium level of cooking under low pressure. It is commonly found in mica schists. It is part of a three-mineral family, along with kyanite and sillimanite.

COLOR Brown, green, white

HARDNESS 6.5–7.5

LUSTER Vitreous

CLEAVAGE/FRACTURE Good

SPECIFIC GRAVITY 3.17

STREAK White

HABIT Normally grows columnar crystals, which have square-shaped cross sections

COMPOSITION Al_2SiO_5 (Aluminum silicate)

MINERAL GROUP Silicates: Single block structure

Flint (flint)

Flint is a hard, very fine-grained variety of quartz. It is found as nodules within sedimentary rocks such as chalk and limestone. It breaks to form curved, sharp edges, which were used in the Stone Age as knives and other tools. When it is struck against steel, flint can create enough sparks to set dry materials or even gunpowder on fire. Technically, it is a rock, but is often treated as a mineral by rock hounds.

COLOR Browns and yellows

HARDNESS 6.5–7.0

LUSTER Waxy

CLEAVAGE/FRACTURE None, fractures in sharp, curved surfaces

SPECIFIC GRAVITY 2.6

STREAK White

HABIT Massive, in nodules

COMPOSITION SiO_2 (Silicon dioxide)

MINERAL GROUP Silicates: Framework structure

Cassiterite (cas–sit–er–ite)

Cassiterite is a major ore of the metal tin. It is mostly found in rivers or old glacial deposits of sediments, but can also be found in veins formed by hot waters or in pegmatites. It also has been used to make beautiful gemstones because of its hardness and luster.

COLOR Brown or black

HARDNESS 6–7

LUSTER Like diamonds, metallic

CLEAVAGE/FRACTURE Can cleave in three directions

SPECIFIC GRAVITY 7.0

STREAK White to brown

HABIT Forms pyramid-shaped crystals and crusts on other minerals

COMPOSITION SnO_2 (Tin oxide)

MINERAL GROUP Oxides and friends

Smoky Quartz (smo–key kworts)

Smoky quartz is a gray to light-brown variety of quartz that you can see through. Sometimes crystals of smoky quartz start almost clear at their tips and get darker as you move down the crystal.

COLOR Brown to gray

HARDNESS 7

LUSTER Vitreous

CLEAVAGE/FRACTURE None, breaks in curved surfaces

SPECIFIC GRAVITY 2.65

STREAK White

HABIT Six-sided prisms ending often in six-sided points

COMPOSITION SiO_2 (Silicon dioxide)

MINERAL GROUP Silicates: Framework structure

Staurolite (stau-ro-lite)

Staurolite is a metamorphic mineral found in gneiss and other high-pressure rocks. It often forms twins that together look like crosses in the rock. These can weather out, so you might find loose crosses of the mineral.

COLOR Brown to black

HARDNESS 7.0–7.5

LUSTER Vitreous, and sometimes like resin

CLEAVAGE/FRACTURE Cleaves on one plane, fractures with rounded surfaces

SPECIFIC GRAVITY 3.8

STREAK White to gray

HABIT Forms twins that appear as crosses

COMPOSITION
$Fe^{2+}_2Al_9O_6(SiO_4)_4(O,OH)_2$ (Iron aluminum hydrated silicate)

MINERAL GROUP Silicates: Single block structure

Corundum (co-run-dum)

Corundum is found in metamorphic rocks and some igneous rocks. It is an extremely hard mineral and is used as an abrasive, often in sandpaper. It has some colored gem varieties such as sapphire and ruby.

COLOR Brown, black, or gray

HARDNESS 9

LUSTER Vitreous

CLEAVAGE/FRACTURE None

SPECIFIC GRAVITY 4.0

STREAK White, but impossible to test because it is so hard

HABIT Six-sided crystals

COMPOSITION Al_2O_3 (Aluminum oxide)

MINERAL GROUP Oxides and friends

Sphalerite (sfal-er-ite)

Sphalerite is an ore mineral of the metal zinc. It is found in places where hot waters have brought zinc into contact with carbonate rocks, and they have reacted. It is found in veins and coatings and even as massive deposits.

COLOR Dark brown to yellow

HARDNESS 3.5–4.0

LUSTER Resinous, greasy, but can also be diamond-like

CLEAVAGE/FRACTURE Perfect, in six directions, and breaks in flat surfaces

SPECIFIC GRAVITY 3.9–4.2

STREAK Pale yellow to white

HABIT Well-formed crystals

COMPOSITION (Zn,Fe)S (Zinc/iron sulfide)

MINERAL GROUP Sulfides and friends

Goethite (go-thite)

Goethite is often called brown iron ore or even bog iron ore. It forms as other iron-rich minerals break down and is the main mineral that people see as rust. It has been used as an ore to make iron. It is a common mineral found around the globe.

COLOR Brown or reddish

HARDNESS 5.0–5.5

LUSTER Dull

CLEAVAGE/FRACTURE Well in one direction, and breaks splintery

SPECIFIC GRAVITY 3.3–4.3

STREAK Brown, sometimes brownish red or yellow

HABIT Forms many shapes from stalactites to small balls

COMPOSITION FeO(OH) (Hydrated iron oxide)

MINERAL GROUP Oxides and friends

Rutile (ru–tile)

Rutile is found in metamorphic and igneous rocks that formed under very high temperatures and pressures. It weathers out and forms part of the minerals that make up heavy beach sands, where it is mined as a source of titanium oxide. It is then used to make plastic and paint white.

COLOR Brown or black

HARDNESS 6.0–6.5

LUSTER Diamond-like to almost metallic

CLEAVAGE/FRACTURE Forms some almost flat surfaces

SPECIFIC GRAVITY 4.23

STREAK Red

HABIT Prism-shaped crystals

COMPOSITION TiO_2 (Titanium oxide)

MINERAL GROUP Oxides and friends

Hematite (he–ma–tite)

See full fact sheet on page 99.

Cuprite (ku-prite)

Cuprite was once used as an ore for the metal copper. It is found in the weathered minerals on top of copper deposits, along with other copper minerals such as azurite and malachite. Cuprite has been used in the past as a gemstone.

COLOR Brown or red

HARDNESS 3.5–4.0

LUSTER Almost metallic

CLEAVAGE/FRACTURE Can break up into eight-sided shapes, fractures unevenly

SPECIFIC GRAVITY 6.14

STREAK Reddish brown

HABIT Can form crystals, but mostly an earthy mass

COMPOSITION Cu_2O (Copper oxide)

MINERAL GROUP Oxides and friends

Titanite (ti-ta-nite)

Titanite, sometimes called sphene, is found as a mineral in quartz-rich igneous rocks and pegmatites. It can also be found in metamorphic rocks, like gneiss and schist. It is not used as a gemstone because it is soft and its crystals are too small.

COLOR Brown, green, yellow

HARDNESS 5.0–5.5

LUSTER Diamond-like to almost waxy

CLEAVAGE/FRACTURE One direction

SPECIFIC GRAVITY 3.5

STREAK Pink

HABIT Massive, sometimes as small flattened crystals

COMPOSITION $CaTiSiO_5$ (Calcium titanium silicate)

MINERAL GROUP Silicates: Single block structure

Garnet (gar-net)

Garnets are a group of minerals used as gemstones and as abrasives. It is the abrasive mineral in many sandpapers! Garnets come in many different colors. They are a sign of metamorphism, often found in rocks involved in mountain building.

COLOR Red, but also green, yellow, violet, and rarely, blue

HARDNESS 6.5–7.5

LUSTER Vitreous

CLEAVAGE/FRACTURE None, breaks in curved faces

SPECIFIC GRAVITY 3.1–4.3

STREAK White

HABIT Twelve-sided crystals

COMPOSITION $(Mg,Fe,Mn,Ca)_3Al_2(SiO_4)_3$ (Complex chemistry with many combinations)

MINERAL GROUP Silicates: Single block structure

Zircon (zir-con)

Zircon is found in igneous rocks. It rarely changes with weathering, heat, or pressure. Because of this, some zircons are the oldest minerals found on the Earth! These specimens are used to help find the age of the rocks in which they are found.

COLOR Red, brown, or yellow

HARDNESS 7.5

LUSTER Vitreous to diamond-like

CLEAVAGE/FRACTURE Good

SPECIFIC GRAVITY 4.6–4.7

STREAK White

HABIT Small tabular crystals, small mineral grains

COMPOSITION $ZrSiO_4$ (Zirconium silicate)

MINERAL GROUP Silicates: Single block structure

Ruby (ru-bee)

Ruby is the red gem variety of the mineral corundum. It can be distinguished by its extreme hardness. Large rubies are very rare, and many contain small substances that can create strange light effects, such as making it look like there are stars inside the stone.

COLOR Red

HARDNESS 9

LUSTER Vitreous

CLEAVAGE/FRACTURE None

SPECIFIC GRAVITY 4.0

STREAK White, but impossible to test because it is so hard

HABIT Forms six-sided crystals

COMPOSITION Al_2O_3 (Aluminum oxide)

MINERAL GROUP Oxides and friends

Realgar (re-al-gar)

Realgar is an ore of arsenic and is often called arsenic ruby. It has been used for firewood and even as a weed poison. It is a toxic mineral that should not be handled if you come across it. It is safe in an enclosed jar.

COLOR Red

HARDNESS 1.5–2.0

LUSTER Resinous or greasy

CLEAVAGE/FRACTURE Can cleave in a few directions

SPECIFIC GRAVITY 3.56

STREAK Red to orange

HABIT Forms prism-shaped crystals, but can be fine-grained or massive

COMPOSITION AsS (Arsenic sulfide)

MINERAL GROUP Sulfides and friends

Cinnabar (ci-na-bar)

Cinnabar is the major ore of the liquid metal mercury. In historical times, it was also used to make a deep red dye that was called vermillion. Cinnabar is found in veins in recent volcanic rocks and around hot springs. It is a mineral that must be handled carefully because mercury is poisonous. If you find some, just take a photo of it and leave it alone. Any samples, however, should be stored and displayed in a closed jar.

COLOR Red

HARDNESS 2.0–2.5

LUSTER Diamond-like to dull

CLEAVAGE/FRACTURE
Forms prisms when broken

SPECIFIC GRAVITY 8.1

STREAK Red

HABIT Mostly granular or as crusts on other minerals

COMPOSITION HgS (Mercury sulfide)

MINERAL GROUP Sulfides and friends

Cuprite (ku-prite)

See full fact sheet on page 114.

ROCKS

Granite (gran-it)

Granite is used as a building stone because it is hard and durable. It is now often used for gravestones! Granite is often found as the core of eroded mountain ranges.

COLOR Light gray and light pink

MINERALS Quartz, orthoclase, plagioclase, biotite, and muscovite

GRAIN SIZE Large interlocking crystals up to half an inch (1.25 cm) in size, and may contain some larger feldspar crystals

ORIGIN Forms from the cooling of silica-rich molten rock and cools slowly, allowing large crystals to form.

CLASSIFICATION Igneous: plutonic, felsic

Tonalite (toe-nal-ite)

Tonalite is an igneous rock that is similar to granite, but is darker in color and contains mostly plagioclase.

COLOR Gray, sometimes with a green tinge

MINERALS Plagioclase, biotite, mica, hornblende, pyroxene, and sometimes quartz

GRAIN SIZE Large interlocking crystals up to half an inch (1.25 cm) in size, and may contain some larger feldspar crystals

ORIGIN Forms from the cooling of molten rock and cools slowly, allowing large crystals to form.

CLASSIFICATION Igneous: plutonic, felsic

Monzonite (mon-zo-nite)

Monzonite has two types of feldspar in equal amounts, which is unusual. It sometimes contains enough copper to become copper ore. It has been used to build some famous buildings in the US, including the Mormon temple in Salt Lake City, Utah.

COLOR Pale cream, gray, or pink

MINERALS Plagioclase and orthoclase, small amounts of quartz, biotite, and hornblende

GRAIN SIZE Large interlocking crystals up to half an inch (1.25 cm) in size, and may contain some larger feldspar crystals

ORIGIN Forms from the cooling of molten rock and cools slowly, allowing large crystals to form.

CLASSIFICATION Igneous: plutonic, felsic

Pegmatite (peg-ma-tite)

Pegmatites are awesome places to find large mineral specimens. It has been mined not only for gem minerals, including tourmaline and emeralds, but also for mica and feldspar. In some places, crystals as large as cars have been found in pegmatite!

COLOR White, light gray, or pink

MINERALS Mostly quartz, feldspar, and mica, but also tourmaline, beryl, garnets, and many more rare and exotic minerals

GRAIN SIZE Very large crystals

ORIGIN Normally found with granite, and it forms from the slow cooling of mineral rock fluids in cracks and fractures in rocks.

CLASSIFICATION Igneous: plutonic, felsic

Porphyry (por-fe-ree)

Almost more a texture than an actual rock type, porphyry contains large crystals, like feldspar, in a fine-grained rock. Sometimes, the large crystals show banding called **zoning** that tells how the large crystals grew. Porphyry has been widely used as ornamental building stones.

COLOR Various

MINERALS Feldspar or quartz

GRAIN SIZE Large crystals in fine grains

ORIGIN Forms when crystals start to grow slowly in a cooling pool of molten rock, which then cools quickly, locking those larger crystals into a finer rock.

CLASSIFICATION Igneous: plutonic, felsic

Granodiorite (grano-di-o-rite)

If you took all the rocks on all the continents, ground them up, and worked out the total chemistry, it would be the same as granodiorite!

COLOR Medium to dark gray

MINERALS Plagioclase, orthoclase, quartz, and mica

GRAIN SIZE Large interlocking crystals up to half an inch (1.25 cm) in size, and may contain some larger feldspar

ORIGIN Forms from the cooling of silica-rich molten rock deep in the Earth's crust and cools slowly, allowing large crystals to form.

CLASSIFICATION Igneous: plutonic, intermediate

Syenite (sigh-e-nite)

Syenite looks very similar to granite, but quartz normally makes up less than 5% of syenite.

COLOR Gray or cream

MINERALS Orthoclase, small amounts of plagioclase, hornblende, pyroxene, and, in very small amounts, quartz

GRAIN SIZE Large interlocking crystals up to half an inch (1.25 cm) in size, and may contain some larger feldspar crystals

ORIGIN Forms when granite is partially remelted deep in the crust and the melted rock then recrystallizes slowly to form large crystals.

CLASSIFICATION Igneous: plutonic, intermediate

Diorite (di-o-rite)

This is an igneous rock that falls in composition between granite and gabbro. Diorite is a very hard rock that is hard to carve but takes a very high polish and many of the famous statues of Egypt are made of this rock.

COLOR Gray to black.

MINERALS Plagioclase feldspar, pyroxene, olivine and amphibole; can even contain small amounts of quartz.

GRAIN SIZE & TEXTURE Large interlocking crystals up to half an inch in size. It can also have a speckled texture with light colored feldspars with darker other minerals.

ORIGIN Formed from the melting of rocks like gabbro.

CLASSIFICATION Igneous-plutonic-intermediate

Gabbro (gab-bro)

The Earth's ocean floors are made up of basalt on top of a thick layer of gabbro. Sometimes, old ocean floor is pushed up and onto land during mountain building in a place where we can see and collect gabbro.

COLOR Dark gray to dark green

MINERALS Plagioclase, pyroxene, olivine, and amphibole

GRAIN SIZE Large inter-locking crystals up to half an inch (1.25 cm) in size

ORIGIN Gabbro forms from the cooling of molten rock underneath the Earth's ocean crust and cools slowly, allow-ing large crystals to form.

CLASSIFICATION Igneous: plutonic, mafic

Peridotite (pe-ri-do-tite)

Peridotite is made up of basically two minerals and is thought to be the rock that makes up the mantle, the Earth's thickest layer. In some places, ancient parts of the mantle have been thrust up by moun-tain building, and peridotite has been exposed.

COLOR Dark green

MINERALS Olivine and pyroxene

GRAIN SIZE Coarse- to medium-grained crystals

ORIGIN This is mantle material that has been brought up to the Earth's surface by plate tectonic collisions or by some volcanic eruptions.

CLASSIFICATION Igneous: plutonic, ultra-mafic

Carbonatite (car-bon-a-tite)

Carbonatite is a very special type of igneous rock because it is *not* made up of the normal silicate minerals; instead, it is made up of carbonate minerals. Carbonatite is rare, but people love to have it in their collections. Carbonatite is often mistaken for marble!

COLOR Light gray or white

MINERALS Sodalite, apatite, magnetite, barite, fluorite, and some silicate minerals like mica

GRAIN SIZE Coarse- to medium-grained interlocking crystals

ORIGIN Carbonatite is rare and seems to form where tectonic plates are pulling apart on land.

CLASSIFICATION Igneous: plutonic, carbonates

Picrite (pic-rite)

Picrite is a special type of basalt. It is found as lava flows on oceanic island volcanoes, in places like Hawaii, in the Pacific Ocean, or Reunion Island, in the Indian Ocean.

COLOR Black or dark gray with green crystals

MINERALS Olivine, plagioclase, augite, and hornblende

GRAIN SIZE Large olivine crystals

ORIGIN Picrite is formed in lava flows from ocean island volcanoes.

CLASSIFICATION Igneous: volcanic, mafic

Ignimbrite (ig-nim-brite)

Ignimbrite is a type of volcanic rock that forms from a deadly type of gas-rich eruption event known as a pyroclastic flow. Ignimbrite can have very thick layers that are resistant to weathering and, therefore, forms ridges and mountains well after the volcanoes have eroded away. Because of the way ignimbrite forms, it can contain fragments of volcanic or even pluton-ic rock all welded together in a finer material. Those fragments are normally intermediate to felsic igneous in composition.

COLOR White, pink, cream, brown, or gray

MINERALS Quartz, felspar, and mica

GRAIN SIZE Mixed

ORIGIN Forms from pyroclastic flows around explosive volcanoes.

CLASSIFICATION Igneous: volcanic, felsic, intermediate

Scoria (score-ee-a)

Scoria is the name given to fragments of volcanic rock. Some propane barbecue grills have a layer of scoria inside them to even out the cooking heat. Scoria contains lots of bubbles and holes. While it can be light-weight, it does not float on water like pumice.

COLOR Light gray, red, or brown

MINERALS Depends on the type of volcano

GRAIN SIZE Mixed

ORIGIN Forms from volcanic material from eruptions and can be molten material that cools when shot into the air by fountains of lava.

CLASSIFICATION Igneous: volcanic mafic, felsic

Pyroclastic (Pi-ro-clas-tic)

Pyroclastic is not a rock but rock fragments found around volcanoes. Its name means "fire frag-ments." It includes things like cinder, scoria, ash, and pumice that build up on the slopes of a volcano. These grains can be shaped like tears, spindles, and even hair!

COLOR Reds, brown, black, and cream

MINERALS Olivine and feldspar

GRAIN SIZE Mixed

ORIGIN Forms from the volcano eruption of molten rock materials into the air, where it cools before it falls to the ground in loose materi-als, or it can sometimes be pulverized rock that a volcano has exploded into the air.

CLASSIFICATION Igneous: volcanic, mafic, felsic

Andesite (an-des-ite)

Andesite is a volcanic rock that forms the steep-sided composite volcanoes of the world, like the Andean Volcanic Belt in the Andes Mountains of South America—which gives the rock its name—and the Cascade volcanoes in the Pacific Northwest of the United States.

COLOR Light gray to light brown

MINERALS Plagioclase, pyroxenes, hornblende, and sometimes quartz

GRAIN SIZE Very fine-grained crystals hard to see with the naked eye, but occasionally some larger crystals

ORIGIN Forms steep-sided composite volcanoes around the world.

CLASSIFICATION Igneous: volcanic, intermediate

Trachyte (tra-kite)

Trachyte is a type of volcanic rock that contains loads of orthoclase.

COLOR Pale gray

MINERALS Orthoclase, small amounts of plagioclase and quartz, and sometimes biotite and olivine

GRAIN SIZE Very fine-grained and often hard to see with the naked eye

ORIGIN Forms as thick, slow-moving lava flows from certain volcanoes.

CLASSIFICATION Igneous: volcanic, intermediate

Tuff (tuff)

Tuff is the rock that forms when volcanic ash settles and hardens into rock. It can form very thick layers close to a volcano, which then thin out as you move farther away from the volcano vent. Some volcanic eruptions in the past have blanketed huge areas with volcanic ash, and those tuff beds can be mapped for hundreds of miles (kilometers) from the source. Tuff, despite its name, is soft to work with and has been used as building stones.

COLOR Light gray or brown to light cream

MINERALS Depends on the type of volcano

GRAIN SIZE Very fine, powder-size particles too small to see with the naked eye

ORIGIN Forms from volcanic ash from large explosive eruptions.

CLASSIFICATION Igneous: volcanic, felsic, mafic

Dacite (day-site)

Dacite is a volcanic rock that has a mineral makeup between andesite and rhyolite. It is found around volcanoes that can be explosive, where it clogs up the volcano's eruptive pipes until pressure blows the dacite out.

COLOR Light gray to cream

MINERALS Plagioclase, biotite, quartz, hornblende, and augite

GRAIN SIZE Very fine-grained and hard to see with the naked eye, but occasionally larger crystals

ORIGIN Mostly forms on explosive volcanoes and in places where molten rock "evolves" over time in a magma chamber.

CLASSIFICATION Igneous: volcanic, intermediate

Basalt (ba-salt)

Basalt is a volcanic rock formed from the cooling of lava from shield volcanoes like those in Hawaii. It *never* contains quartz, but it can contain visible crystals of olivine.

COLOR Black to dark gray

MINERALS Olivine, plagioclase, augite, and hornblende

GRAIN SIZE Very fine-grained and hard to see with the naked eye, but occasionally larger crystals

ORIGIN Forms from the cooling of lava at shield volcanoes and at most underwater volcanoes, and, sometimes, old basalt flows cap the top of hills.

CLASSIFICATION Igneous: volcanic, mafic

Pumice (pum-iss)

Pumice is an air-filled volcanic rock that is so light, it can float on water! It will often travel long distances in the ocean and be washed up on beaches thousands of miles (kilometers) away from the volcano where it formed. Pumice is often sold as an abrasive.

COLOR Pale gray or cream

MINERALS None visible

GRAIN SIZE Fine-grained mass full of holes and bubbles

ORIGIN Forms from the eruptions of explosive volcanoes with a high silica content.

CLASSIFICATION Igneous: volcanic, felsic

Rhyolite (rye-o-lite)

Rhyolite is a hard, silica-rich, volcanic rock that, when still molten, is very thick and hardly flows, often forming lava domes. Sometimes rhyolite has banding.

COLOR Pale gray, pale pink, or pale brown

MINERALS Quartz, feldspar, and mica

GRAIN SIZE Very fine-grained and often not visible to the naked eye, but you may occasionally see some larger ones with the naked eye

ORIGIN Can be found in areas long after a land volcano has eroded away.

CLASSIFICATION Igneous: volcanic, felsic

Obsidian (ob-sid-i-an)

Obsidian is volcanic glass found on the edges of rhyolite flows. It is made up of the same chemicals as rhyolite, but none of the elements form crystals.. In the past, obsidian was used a lot for arrowheads and other stone tools, and it is still used today for some scalpel blades.

COLOR Black or very dark green

MINERALS Quartz, feldspar, and mica

GRAIN SIZE None

ORIGIN When a lava flow has a very high silica content, the edges of the flow cool before the elements can form crystals, and that's how a glass-like obsidian is formed.

CLASSIFICATION Igneous: volcanic, felsic

Conglomerate (con-glom-er-ate)

A conglomerate rock contains large chunks of other rocks that have been cemented together naturally with finer materials like sand and mud. The shape of conglomerate rock fragments can tell us how much energy the water had to roll the rocks around before they were cemented together.

COLOR Browns, reds, and grays

GRAIN SIZE An inch (2.5 cm) or larger

ORIGIN Form in watery places where large rock pieces can accumulate, such as in rivers, glacier moraines, or talus slopes.

Breccia (breh-cha)

Breccia is very similar to conglomerate rock except that breccia's large rock fragments are very angular. It is common in areas where earthquakes and even volcanic eruptions take place. Breccia is also found near meteor impact craters.

COLOR Mostly dark browns, grays, and greens

GRAIN SIZE Large, an inch (2.5 cm) or greater, surrounded by small grains

ORIGIN Forms when rocks are broken up or crushed because of the Earth's movements, including earthquakes, or a violent steam eruption, which shatters surrounding rocks.

Oil Shale (oil shale)

Similar to shale, oil shale has the amazing property of being able to release oil when treated! This is because oil shale is a mix of organic compounds made up of the remains of microscopic plants and animals. Oil shale deposits occur around the globe.

COLOR Dark gray to gray

GRAIN SIZE Fine-size

ORIGIN Forms in oceans and lakes where microscopic plants and animals die and become trapped in the mud.

Graywacke (gray-wack)

Often called "dirty sand-stone," this rock is between shale and sand-stone. Often graywacke contains fragments of ground-up rocks, and while very rare, it can even contain fossils!

COLOR Dark gray, brown, yellow, or black

GRAIN SIZE Sand- and mud-size fragments, all cemented together

ORIGIN Forms when sand and mud are mixed together, mostly as a result of under-water landslides that cause all sediment to travel down to the ocean floor.

Shale (shale)

Shale is a rock that is often ground up to make clay for bricks or tiles or even pottery. Sometimes shale contains awesome fossil layers that can include leaves, ferns, shells, and even fish fossils!

COLOR Mostly gray, with green, pale gray, cream, or white

GRAIN SIZE Very fine-grained to clay-size

ORIGIN Forms from the settling of mud in oceans, bays, or lakes.

Sandstone (sand-stone)

Sandstone is made up of sand-size grains that have been cemented together naturally. The sand grains can be all of one mineral, multiple minerals, or rock fragments. Sandstone grains can form thin layers, be massive, or even show features like cross bedding.

COLOR Yellow, brown, gray, and red

GRAIN SIZE Sand-size

ORIGIN Can form from sand in oceans, lakes, rivers, beaches, and sand dunes, and even windblown sand from glacial areas.

Diatomite (di-at-o-mite)

Diatomite is often mined and crushed up to form a material called diatomaceous earth, or more simply, DE. When you examine diatomite under a microscope, you can see small glassy shards and shells. DE is used for many things including filtering water and even sprinkling on animals to stop fleas!

COLOR White or cream

GRAIN SIZE Extremely fine-grained

ORIGIN Forms on the ocean floor from the silica shells of microscopic algae called diatoms. When the diatoms die, their shells fall through the ocean water and form a sludge, which can turn into rock.

Chert (churt)

Chert is often found replacing fossil materials such as wood to form petrified wood, and it is also found as nodules or blobs inside of other rocks.

COLOR Grays, yellows, reds, or browns

GRAIN SIZE Extremely fine-grained

ORIGIN Most forms from the silica shells of microscopic animals called diatoms, which fall to the ocean floor and accumulate. Some chert dissolves in fluids that move through sedimentary rocks and then recrystallizes out, replacing wood or other organic remains.

Limestone (lime-stone)

Limestone is made up almost entirely of carbonate minerals like calcite or dolomite, and it is part of a group called carbonate rocks. Limestone can be chemically weathered to form amazing caves and caverns full of features like pillars. It often contains lots of fossils.

COLOR White, cream, or gray

GRAIN SIZE Mostly fine-grained, but can have veins of recrystallized calcite

ORIGIN Mostly forms from the shells of living sea creatures like corals. It can also form from limy mud in lagoons near coral reefs or even as sludge on the ocean floor that is chemically formed from the water.

Oolite (oo-lite)

This carbonate rock is made up of millions of small round balls called ooliths. Oolite is often mined and ground up to be used in aquarium filters.

COLOR White or cream

GRAIN SIZE Small balls of calcium carbonate or other minerals

ORIGIN Forms from the depositing of calcium carbonate or other minerals on the bottoms of shallow lakes or oceans where the water was mineral-rich and moved backward and forward, allowing the minerals to form small round shapes.

Chalk (chok)

Chalk is a special form of limestone. Chalk is also used to produce lime—a chemical used in farming and in making cement. Under a microscope you can see that chalk grains are all shells of tiny animals. These animals die and shed their shells in the ocean. The shells sink to form a layer on the ocean floor. This layer becomes chalk when hardened.

COLOR White or pale cream

GRAIN SIZE Very fine-grained

ORIGIN Forms from the accumulation of millions and millions of tiny shells from coccolithophores.

Laterite (lat-er-ite)

Laterite is sometimes called a soil as well as a rock. It is crushed up and used in some places as a landscape rock because of its rich colors. It has also been used as a source of iron ore, because it is made up of different iron minerals. Laterite is normally made up of small balls and nodules, which can be loose or welded.

COLOR Reds, yellows, and browns

GRAIN SIZE Very fine-grained

ORIGIN Laterite is thought to form from the deep weathering of underlying rocks in hot, wet tropical conditions.

Anthracite (an-thra-site)

Anthracite, or black coal, is the highest quality of coal. It has been mined around the world to be burned to fuel factories, steam trains, and heat homes. It has even been polished to form the mineral-like gemstone jet. Sometimes, anthracite contains small layers of mud, and its layers contain plant fossils or the metallic mineral pyrite.

COLOR Black, often shiny

GRAIN SIZE Fine-grained

ORIGIN Forms from plant material that falls into swamps or wetlands and gets buried there.

Lignite (lig-nite)

Lignite is considered the lowest quality of coal and is often referred to as "brown coal." It is mined and used as fuel for coal-fired power stations around the world. Sometimes it is compressed into pellets or bricks. Lignite is fine-grained, often with layers of mud, which sometimes can contain plant fossils.

COLOR Brown

GRAIN SIZE Fine-grained

ORIGIN Forms from plant material that falls into swamps or wetlands and is buried.

Banded Iron Formation
(band–ed iron for–ma–tion)

Often just called BIF, banded iron formations are all extremely old. The bands are thin and made up of iron-rich mineral layers between layers of muds and sand. More than half of all the iron ore on the Earth occurs in BIF.

COLOR Reds, browns, or yellows

GRAIN SIZE Very fine-grained

ORIGIN It is thought that BIF formed when organisms evolved that produced oxygen as part of life. That oxygen reacted with iron dissolved in the ocean, forming iron minerals that crystallized out and fell to the ocean floor.

Bauxite (box–ite)

Bauxite is an aluminum-rich rock and is the world's largest supply of aluminum ore. It is a mixture of complex aluminum oxide minerals with some iron minerals thrown in. Bauxite often has ball-like layered blobs that make it look a little like a conglomerate.

COLOR Cream, red, and brown

GRAIN SIZE Fine-grained

ORIGIN Scientists are still debating how bauxite forms. It seems to be formed by the weathering of other rocks in tropical conditions.

Gneiss (nice)

Gneiss is formed when almost any rock is placed under very high temperatures and pressures. Unlike many other metamorphic rocks, mica is *not* one of its major minerals.

COLOR Gray or cream, with dark banding

MINERALS Quartz, feldspar, biotite, pyroxene, hornblende, and possibly garnet

GRAIN SIZE Very coarse-grained

ORIGIN Formed from igneous or sedimentary rocks, all cooked under high temperatures and pressures that occur during mountain building.

Amphibolite (am-fib-o-lite)

Amphibolites contain many dark and green minerals and can polish up so well that they are often used to make countertops. They sometimes contain small, well-formed, red garnets.

COLOR Dark green and dark browns

MINERALS Hornblende, biotite, augite, andalusite, kyanite, and sometimes garnet

GRAIN SIZE Coarse-grained

ORIGIN Formed from mafic igneous rocks or clay-rich sediments cooked under pressure during mountain building.

Migmatite (mig–ma–tite)

Migmatite forms when heat and pressure become so great that parts of the original rock have actually melted and other parts metamorphosed. Because of this, migmatite is halfway between an igneous and a metamorphic rock. Migmatite is often considered so pretty that it is cut for countertops and building stones. The rock often shows many colors of banding with crazy twisted folds and veining. Sometimes these bands abruptly end and look like granite.

COLOR Medium gray, pinkish, or green

MINERALS Muscovite, feldspar, quartz, biotite, and amphiboles

GRAIN SIZE Coarse-grained

ORIGIN Could almost form from any rock, with the possible exception of limestone, cooked under very high heat.

Schist (shist)

Schist is one of the prettiest metamorphic rocks, because it sparkles in the sunlight due to it containing a lot of large mica crystals. All the mica in schist is large—¼ inch (5 mm) or more—and it all lines up in pressure bands. The rock tends to break along these pressure bands. Schist belongs to the same family of metamorphic rocks as slate and phyllite.

COLOR Golden yellow, white, or black

MINERALS Muscovite or biotite, and possibly layers of other minerals like quartz, feldspar, and sometimes garnet

GRAIN SIZE Medium- to coarse-grained

ORIGIN Formed from shale cooked under great pressure.

Marble (mar–bel)

Marble was probably the most common building stone in ancient times. It was used for the world's most famous sculptures. Marble is a soft rock that is used around the world. You'll find it in all the major world cities as columns, statues, and fountains.

COLOR White, light gray, or cream

MINERALS Calcite as the major mineral, with other minor minerals

GRAIN SIZE Medium- to coarse-grained interlocking calcite crystals

ORIGIN Formed from limestone that has been cooked up and may have been under pressure.

Quartzite (kwort–site)

Quartzite is an extremely hard rock that has been used as a building stone in many places around the world. It also makes up the crushed rocks found along railway tracks.

COLOR White, pale yellow, and pink

MINERALS Quartz

GRAIN SIZE Finely inter-locking crystals

ORIGIN Formed from quartz-rich sandstone that has been cooked up so that the sand grains all fuse together.

Hornfels (horn–fels)

Hornfels are hard, fine-grained rocks that form from the cooking up of layers of sedimentary rocks mostly when a nearby large body of molten rock, like granite, has intruded into the area.

COLOR Dark gray and greens, but can be pale colors

MINERALS Depends on the original rock

GRAIN SIZE Fine-grained, and normally not visible to the naked eye

ORIGIN Formed when sedimentary rocks are cooked, but not under pressure.

Slate (slate)

Slate has been used as a building stone in some parts of the world for thousands of years. It's most commonly used for roofing, but it has also been used for walls of buildings. Slate often contains fossils, which is unusual for a metamorphic rock. It is in the same family of metamorphic rocks as phyllite and schist.

COLOR Black, dark grays, or greens

MINERALS Quartz and mica

GRAIN SIZE Fine-grained crystals

ORIGIN Formed from shale that has been put under low-grade pressure.

Phyllite (fi-lite)

Phyllite is a fine-grained rock that, when moved around in sunlight, will show a sheen or a shimmer as the light catches bands of mica minerals. It is in the same family of metamorphic rocks as slate and schist.

COLOR Gray and brown

MINERALS Mica and other minerals too small to identify

GRAIN SIZE Very fine-grained

ORIGIN Formed from shale cooked up under medium pressure.

Serpentinite (sir–pen–tin–ite)

Serpentinite is a slippery rock that forms from the metamorphism of mafic igneous rocks like basalt. It is named for its appearance—it sometimes looks like the skin of a snake! Serpentinite is often found close to large fault zones.

COLOR Deep to light green

MINERALS Antigorite, lizardite, chrysotile, and other serpentine minerals

GRAIN SIZE Fine-grained

ORIGIN Forms from mafic to ultra-mafic igneous rocks cooked under low heat and medium pressure.

Soapstone (soap–stone)

Soapstone is actually a form of schist where instead of mica you find talc. Soapstone has been used to carve ornaments for thousands of years, and it has also been used to cover the outside of fireplaces. It is soft and has a slippery or soapy texture.

COLOR Light green to white

MINERALS Talc and tremolite

GRAIN SIZE Very fine-grained

ORIGIN Formed from mafic and ultra-mafic rocks that are cooked up with water and under pressure like where tectonic plates collide.

My Field Notebook

Part of being a rock and mineral detective is remembering to record data about each sample you collect. And this will help you get started! This notebook section is a great place for you to keep a record of your "evidence." This "evidence" will be helpful whenever you are looking at your samples and will remind you of not only what you found, but also where and how you found it!

How to Use This Notebook

Even if you don't know yet what you have found, you need to record some important information about where and how you found a specimen. You will need this to help you with specific identification of specimens, so be as clear and accurate as you can be! Please note that you should use a pencil instead of a pen when recording your information in case you need to make any changes later, based on the identification tests you will perform. If you are treasure hunting with a phone or camera, you can also take photos of the specimens you find in the locations you find them before you collect them.

The following fields of information appear on each notebook page:

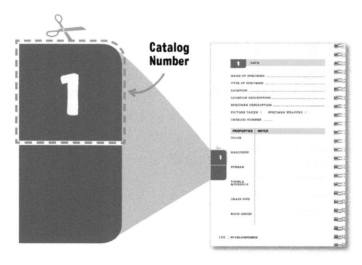

Catalog Number

CATALOG NUMBER

The *most* important thing you need to do is number your sample. A number from 1 to 50 appears on the blue tab of each notebook page. Cut out the number and place it in the plastic bag or egg carton tray, or even glue it onto your collected sample. The second number, which appears at the top of each notebook page, does *not* get cut out. This way, when you go back to your specimen later to do your tests, you'll be sure that you're using the information that corresponds with the correct sample. Please remember: DO THIS PART FIRST!

DATE

List the date when you found this specimen.

NAME OF SPECIMEN

Although this field appears first, you might not be able to fill it in right away. In fact, naming your specimen might be the very last thing you do! I still have samples that have no name. If you have a guess, you can list that guess (again, remember to use a pencil and indicate that this is just a guess). Note that you might have to go back and change this if you end up identifying the specimen as something else entirely after testing. If you don't have a guess, that's okay, too. Just leave it blank!

TYPE OF SPECIMEN

List whether you think a specimen is a rock or a mineral in this section. Again, you might need to change this after you perform identification tests.

LOCATION

The best way to indicate your location is to give a latitude and longitude. This is what a GPS provides, and now most smartphones have an application that will provide latitude and longitude for you. Latitude and longitude coordinates will look like this: 44°00'29.6"N 70°35'38.2"W or 44.008229, –70.593944. Locations north of the equator are positive, those south of the equator are negative. Locations east of London, United Kingdom, are positive, and those west of London, United Kingdom, are negative.

LOCATION DESCRIPTION

Write down the name of the place, like Jones Quarry or Quarry Road. Add some description of exactly where you found the specimen. For example, "two miles past the turn off to Wiley Road, on the left-hand side road cutting." You can also indicate what the terrain is like: Is it very rocky? Are you in the desert? If you can, take a photo of where you found the sample.

SPECIMEN DESCRIPTION

Record how you found the specimen. Was it part of the **bedrock** that you broke off? Was it a loose sample on a **mine dump**? This will provide you some evidence of how that rock was when you collected it, and it could be important when identifying your samples. If you can, take a photo of your sample.

PICTURE TAKEN

Check this box if you were able to take a photo of this specimen and/or its location. Indicate where that photo can be found.

SPECIMEN WRAPPED

Check this box if you were able to wrap your sample.

PROPERTIES TABLE

You will also see a table that includes all of the properties for both rocks and minerals. You will use this to take notes on your findings when you perform identification tests.

You might be wondering: Why is this all so important? You will be collecting rocks and minerals all your life and may one day want to go back to a place that you visited before. Having all this information will help you do that. A latitude and longitude will help you find a place even if the roads have all changed or a forest has grown where there was a clearing. This is especially true if it is a location deep in the woods. When you have filled up this notebook, you can start another one, using all the same fields of information . . . and start the numbering of your samples with 51.

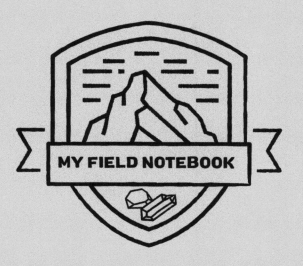

MY FIELD NOTEBOOK

1 DATE:

NAME OF SPECIMEN: _____

TYPE OF SPECIMEN: _____

LOCATION: _____

LOCATION DESCRIPTION: _____

SPECIMEN DESCRIPTION: _____

PICTURE TAKEN ▦   SPECIMEN WRAPPED ▦

CATALOG NUMBER _____

PROPERTIES	NOTES
COLOR	
HARDNESS	
STREAK	
VISIBLE MINERALS	
GRAIN SIZE	
ROCK GROUP	

2 DATE:

NAME OF SPECIMEN: _____

TYPE OF SPECIMEN: _____

LOCATION: _____

LOCATION DESCRIPTION: _____

SPECIMEN DESCRIPTION: _____

PICTURE TAKEN ▪   SPECIMEN WRAPPED ▪

CATALOG NUMBER _____

PROPERTIES	NOTES
COLOR	
HARDNESS	
STREAK	
VISIBLE MINERALS	
GRAIN SIZE	
ROCK GROUP	

2

3 DATE:

NAME OF SPECIMEN: _____

TYPE OF SPECIMEN: _____

LOCATION: _____

LOCATION DESCRIPTION: _____

SPECIMEN DESCRIPTION: _____

PICTURE TAKEN ▨   SPECIMEN WRAPPED ▨

CATALOG NUMBER _____

PROPERTIES	NOTES
COLOR	
HARDNESS	
STREAK	
VISIBLE MINERALS	
GRAIN SIZE	
ROCK GROUP	

4 DATE:

NAME OF SPECIMEN: _____

TYPE OF SPECIMEN: _____

LOCATION: _____

LOCATION DESCRIPTION: _____

SPECIMEN DESCRIPTION: _____

PICTURE TAKEN ▢   SPECIMEN WRAPPED ▢

CATALOG NUMBER _____

PROPERTIES	NOTES
COLOR	
HARDNESS	
STREAK	
VISIBLE MINERALS	
GRAIN SIZE	
ROCK GROUP	

4

5

DATE:

NAME OF SPECIMEN: _____

TYPE OF SPECIMEN: _____

LOCATION: _____

LOCATION DESCRIPTION: _____

SPECIMEN DESCRIPTION: _____

PICTURE TAKEN ▫   SPECIMEN WRAPPED ▫

CATALOG NUMBER _____

PROPERTIES	NOTES
COLOR	
HARDNESS	
STREAK	
VISIBLE MINERALS	
GRAIN SIZE	
ROCK GROUP	

5

6 DATE:

NAME OF SPECIMEN: _____

TYPE OF SPECIMEN: _____

LOCATION: _____

LOCATION DESCRIPTION: _____

SPECIMEN DESCRIPTION: _____

PICTURE TAKEN ■   SPECIMEN WRAPPED ■

CATALOG NUMBER _____

PROPERTIES	NOTES
COLOR	
HARDNESS	
STREAK	
VISIBLE MINERALS	
GRAIN SIZE	
ROCK GROUP	

6

7 DATE:

NAME OF SPECIMEN: _____

TYPE OF SPECIMEN: _____

LOCATION: _____

LOCATION DESCRIPTION: _____

SPECIMEN DESCRIPTION: _____

PICTURE TAKEN ▪   SPECIMEN WRAPPED ▪

CATALOG NUMBER _____

PROPERTIES	NOTES
COLOR	
HARDNESS	
STREAK	
VISIBLE MINERALS	
GRAIN SIZE	
ROCK GROUP	

7

8 DATE:

NAME OF SPECIMEN: _____

TYPE OF SPECIMEN: _____

LOCATION: _____

LOCATION DESCRIPTION: _____

SPECIMEN DESCRIPTION: _____

PICTURE TAKEN ▣   SPECIMEN WRAPPED ▣

CATALOG NUMBER _____

PROPERTIES	NOTES
COLOR	
HARDNESS	
STREAK	
VISIBLE MINERALS	
GRAIN SIZE	
ROCK GROUP	

8

9   DATE:

NAME OF SPECIMEN: _____

TYPE OF SPECIMEN: _____

LOCATION: _____

LOCATION DESCRIPTION: _____

SPECIMEN DESCRIPTION: _____

PICTURE TAKEN ▦   SPECIMEN WRAPPED ▦

CATALOG NUMBER _____

PROPERTIES	NOTES
COLOR	
HARDNESS	
STREAK	
VISIBLE MINERALS	
GRAIN SIZE	
ROCK GROUP	

10 DATE:

NAME OF SPECIMEN: _____

TYPE OF SPECIMEN: _____

LOCATION: _____

LOCATION DESCRIPTION: _____

SPECIMEN DESCRIPTION: _____

PICTURE TAKEN ▢   SPECIMEN WRAPPED ▢

CATALOG NUMBER _____

PROPERTIES	NOTES
COLOR	
HARDNESS	
STREAK	
VISIBLE MINERALS	
GRAIN SIZE	
ROCK GROUP	

10

11 DATE:

NAME OF SPECIMEN: _____

TYPE OF SPECIMEN: _____

LOCATION: _____

LOCATION DESCRIPTION: _____

SPECIMEN DESCRIPTION: _____

PICTURE TAKEN ▪   SPECIMEN WRAPPED ▪

CATALOG NUMBER _____

PROPERTIES	NOTES
COLOR	
HARDNESS	
STREAK	
VISIBLE MINERALS	
GRAIN SIZE	
ROCK GROUP	

12

DATE: _____

NAME OF SPECIMEN: _____

TYPE OF SPECIMEN: _____

LOCATION: _____

LOCATION DESCRIPTION: _____

SPECIMEN DESCRIPTION: _____

PICTURE TAKEN ☐   SPECIMEN WRAPPED ☐

CATALOG NUMBER _____

PROPERTIES	NOTES
COLOR	
HARDNESS	
STREAK	
VISIBLE MINERALS	
GRAIN SIZE	
ROCK GROUP	

12

13

DATE: _____

NAME OF SPECIMEN: _____

TYPE OF SPECIMEN: _____

LOCATION: _____

LOCATION DESCRIPTION: _____

SPECIMEN DESCRIPTION: _____

PICTURE TAKEN ▪   SPECIMEN WRAPPED ▪

CATALOG NUMBER _____

PROPERTIES	NOTES
COLOR	
HARDNESS	
STREAK	
VISIBLE MINERALS	
GRAIN SIZE	
ROCK GROUP	

14 DATE:

NAME OF SPECIMEN: _____

TYPE OF SPECIMEN: _____

LOCATION: _____

LOCATION DESCRIPTION: _____

SPECIMEN DESCRIPTION: _____

PICTURE TAKEN ▪   SPECIMEN WRAPPED ▪

CATALOG NUMBER _____

PROPERTIES	NOTES
COLOR	
HARDNESS	
STREAK	
VISIBLE MINERALS	
GRAIN SIZE	
ROCK GROUP	

14

15　DATE:

NAME OF SPECIMEN: _____

TYPE OF SPECIMEN: _____

LOCATION: _____

LOCATION DESCRIPTION: _____

SPECIMEN DESCRIPTION: _____

PICTURE TAKEN ■　　SPECIMEN WRAPPED ■

CATALOG NUMBER _____

15

PROPERTIES	NOTES
COLOR	
HARDNESS	
STREAK	
VISIBLE MINERALS	
GRAIN SIZE	
ROCK GROUP	

16 DATE:

NAME OF SPECIMEN: _____

TYPE OF SPECIMEN: _____

LOCATION: _____

LOCATION DESCRIPTION: _____

SPECIMEN DESCRIPTION: _____

PICTURE TAKEN ■   SPECIMEN WRAPPED ■

CATALOG NUMBER _____

PROPERTIES	NOTES
COLOR	
HARDNESS	
STREAK	
VISIBLE MINERALS	
GRAIN SIZE	
ROCK GROUP	

16

17 DATE:

NAME OF SPECIMEN: _____

TYPE OF SPECIMEN: _____

LOCATION: _____

LOCATION DESCRIPTION: _____

SPECIMEN DESCRIPTION: _____

PICTURE TAKEN ▢   SPECIMEN WRAPPED ▢

CATALOG NUMBER _____

PROPERTIES	NOTES
COLOR	
HARDNESS	
STREAK	
VISIBLE MINERALS	
GRAIN SIZE	
ROCK GROUP	

17

18   DATE:

NAME OF SPECIMEN: _____

TYPE OF SPECIMEN: _____

LOCATION: _____

LOCATION DESCRIPTION: _____

SPECIMEN DESCRIPTION: _____

PICTURE TAKEN ▨   SPECIMEN WRAPPED ▨

CATALOG NUMBER _____

PROPERTIES	NOTES
COLOR	
HARDNESS	
STREAK	
VISIBLE MINERALS	
GRAIN SIZE	
ROCK GROUP	

18

19   DATE:

NAME OF SPECIMEN: _____

TYPE OF SPECIMEN: _____

LOCATION: _____

LOCATION DESCRIPTION: _____

SPECIMEN DESCRIPTION: _____

PICTURE TAKEN ▣   SPECIMEN WRAPPED ▣

CATALOG NUMBER _____

PROPERTIES	NOTES
COLOR	
HARDNESS	
STREAK	
VISIBLE MINERALS	
GRAIN SIZE	
ROCK GROUP	

20 DATE:

NAME OF SPECIMEN: _____

TYPE OF SPECIMEN: _____

LOCATION: _____

LOCATION DESCRIPTION: _____

SPECIMEN DESCRIPTION: _____

PICTURE TAKEN ■   SPECIMEN WRAPPED ■

CATALOG NUMBER _____

PROPERTIES	NOTES
COLOR	
HARDNESS	
STREAK	
VISIBLE MINERALS	
GRAIN SIZE	
ROCK GROUP	

20

NAME OF SPECIMEN: _____

TYPE OF SPECIMEN: _____

LOCATION: _____

LOCATION DESCRIPTION: _____

SPECIMEN DESCRIPTION: _____

PICTURE TAKEN ▨   SPECIMEN WRAPPED ▨

CATALOG NUMBER _____

PROPERTIES	NOTES
COLOR	
HARDNESS	
STREAK	
VISIBLE MINERALS	
GRAIN SIZE	
ROCK GROUP	

22   DATE:

NAME OF SPECIMEN: _____

TYPE OF SPECIMEN: _____

LOCATION: _____

LOCATION DESCRIPTION: _____

SPECIMEN DESCRIPTION: _____

PICTURE TAKEN ▦   SPECIMEN WRAPPED ▦

CATALOG NUMBER _____

PROPERTIES	NOTES
COLOR	
HARDNESS	
STREAK	
VISIBLE MINERALS	
GRAIN SIZE	
ROCK GROUP	

22

23 DATE:

NAME OF SPECIMEN: _____

TYPE OF SPECIMEN: _____

LOCATION: _____

LOCATION DESCRIPTION: _____

SPECIMEN DESCRIPTION: _____

PICTURE TAKEN ◾ SPECIMEN WRAPPED ◾

CATALOG NUMBER _____

PROPERTIES	NOTES
COLOR	
HARDNESS	
STREAK	
VISIBLE MINERALS	
GRAIN SIZE	
ROCK GROUP	

24 DATE:

NAME OF SPECIMEN: _____

TYPE OF SPECIMEN: _____

LOCATION: _____

LOCATION DESCRIPTION: _____

SPECIMEN DESCRIPTION: _____

PICTURE TAKEN ▨   SPECIMEN WRAPPED ▨

CATALOG NUMBER _____

PROPERTIES	NOTES
COLOR	
HARDNESS	
STREAK	
VISIBLE MINERALS	
GRAIN SIZE	
ROCK GROUP	

24

25   DATE:

NAME OF SPECIMEN: _____

TYPE OF SPECIMEN: _____

LOCATION: _____

LOCATION DESCRIPTION: _____

SPECIMEN DESCRIPTION: _____

PICTURE TAKEN ▣   SPECIMEN WRAPPED ▣

CATALOG NUMBER _____

PROPERTIES	NOTES
COLOR	
HARDNESS	
STREAK	
VISIBLE MINERALS	
GRAIN SIZE	
ROCK GROUP	

25

26 DATE:

NAME OF SPECIMEN: _____

TYPE OF SPECIMEN: _____

LOCATION: _____

LOCATION DESCRIPTION: _____

SPECIMEN DESCRIPTION: _____

PICTURE TAKEN ▢   SPECIMEN WRAPPED ▢

CATALOG NUMBER _____

PROPERTIES	NOTES
COLOR	
HARDNESS	
STREAK	
VISIBLE MINERALS	
GRAIN SIZE	
ROCK GROUP	

26

27 DATE:

NAME OF SPECIMEN: _____

TYPE OF SPECIMEN: _____

LOCATION: _____

LOCATION DESCRIPTION: _____

SPECIMEN DESCRIPTION: _____

PICTURE TAKEN ☐   SPECIMEN WRAPPED ☐

CATALOG NUMBER _____

PROPERTIES	NOTES
COLOR	
HARDNESS	
STREAK	
VISIBLE MINERALS	
GRAIN SIZE	
ROCK GROUP	

27

NAME OF SPECIMEN: _____

TYPE OF SPECIMEN: _____

LOCATION: _____

LOCATION DESCRIPTION: _____

SPECIMEN DESCRIPTION: _____

PICTURE TAKEN ■   SPECIMEN WRAPPED ■

CATALOG NUMBER _____

PROPERTIES	NOTES
COLOR	
HARDNESS	
STREAK	
VISIBLE MINERALS	
GRAIN SIZE	
ROCK GROUP	

28

29 DATE:

NAME OF SPECIMEN: _____

TYPE OF SPECIMEN: _____

LOCATION: _____

LOCATION DESCRIPTION: _____

SPECIMEN DESCRIPTION: _____

PICTURE TAKEN ■   SPECIMEN WRAPPED ■

CATALOG NUMBER _____

PROPERTIES	NOTES
COLOR	
HARDNESS	
STREAK	
VISIBLE MINERALS	
GRAIN SIZE	
ROCK GROUP	

29

30 DATE:

NAME OF SPECIMEN: _____

TYPE OF SPECIMEN: _____

LOCATION: _____

LOCATION DESCRIPTION: _____

SPECIMEN DESCRIPTION: _____

PICTURE TAKEN ▢   SPECIMEN WRAPPED ▢

CATALOG NUMBER _____

PROPERTIES	NOTES
COLOR	
HARDNESS	
STREAK	
VISIBLE MINERALS	
GRAIN SIZE	
ROCK GROUP	

30

31

DATE:

NAME OF SPECIMEN: _____

TYPE OF SPECIMEN: _____

LOCATION: _____

LOCATION DESCRIPTION: _____

SPECIMEN DESCRIPTION: _____

PICTURE TAKEN ◼   SPECIMEN WRAPPED ◼

CATALOG NUMBER _____

PROPERTIES	NOTES
COLOR	
HARDNESS	
STREAK	
VISIBLE MINERALS	
GRAIN SIZE	
ROCK GROUP	

31

32   DATE:

NAME OF SPECIMEN: _____

TYPE OF SPECIMEN: _____

LOCATION: _____

LOCATION DESCRIPTION: _____

SPECIMEN DESCRIPTION: _____

PICTURE TAKEN ▧   SPECIMEN WRAPPED ▧

CATALOG NUMBER _____

PROPERTIES	NOTES
COLOR	
HARDNESS	
STREAK	
VISIBLE MINERALS	
GRAIN SIZE	
ROCK GROUP	

32

33 DATE:

NAME OF SPECIMEN: _____

TYPE OF SPECIMEN: _____

LOCATION: _____

LOCATION DESCRIPTION: _____

SPECIMEN DESCRIPTION: _____

PICTURE TAKEN ▪   SPECIMEN WRAPPED ▪

CATALOG NUMBER _____

PROPERTIES	NOTES
COLOR	
HARDNESS	
STREAK	
VISIBLE MINERALS	
GRAIN SIZE	
ROCK GROUP	

34 DATE:

NAME OF SPECIMEN: _____

TYPE OF SPECIMEN: _____

LOCATION: _____

LOCATION DESCRIPTION: _____

SPECIMEN DESCRIPTION: _____

PICTURE TAKEN ▣   SPECIMEN WRAPPED ▣

CATALOG NUMBER _____

PROPERTIES	NOTES
COLOR	
HARDNESS	
STREAK	
VISIBLE MINERALS	
GRAIN SIZE	
ROCK GROUP	

34

35 DATE:

NAME OF SPECIMEN: _____

TYPE OF SPECIMEN: _____

LOCATION: _____

LOCATION DESCRIPTION: _____

SPECIMEN DESCRIPTION: _____

PICTURE TAKEN ▧   SPECIMEN WRAPPED ▧

CATALOG NUMBER _____

PROPERTIES	NOTES
COLOR	
HARDNESS	
STREAK	
VISIBLE MINERALS	
GRAIN SIZE	
ROCK GROUP	

36   DATE:

NAME OF SPECIMEN: _____

TYPE OF SPECIMEN: _____

LOCATION: _____

LOCATION DESCRIPTION: _____

SPECIMEN DESCRIPTION: _____

PICTURE TAKEN ▪   SPECIMEN WRAPPED ▪

CATALOG NUMBER _____

PROPERTIES	NOTES
COLOR	
HARDNESS	
STREAK	
VISIBLE MINERALS	
GRAIN SIZE	
ROCK GROUP	

36

37 DATE:

NAME OF SPECIMEN: _____

TYPE OF SPECIMEN: _____

LOCATION: _____

LOCATION DESCRIPTION: _____

SPECIMEN DESCRIPTION: _____

PICTURE TAKEN ▩   SPECIMEN WRAPPED ▩

CATALOG NUMBER _____

PROPERTIES	NOTES
COLOR	
HARDNESS	
STREAK	
VISIBLE MINERALS	
GRAIN SIZE	
ROCK GROUP	

37

38 DATE:

NAME OF SPECIMEN: _____

TYPE OF SPECIMEN: _____

LOCATION: _____

LOCATION DESCRIPTION: _____

SPECIMEN DESCRIPTION: _____

PICTURE TAKEN ▣   SPECIMEN WRAPPED ▣

CATALOG NUMBER _____

PROPERTIES	NOTES
COLOR	
HARDNESS	
STREAK	
VISIBLE MINERALS	
GRAIN SIZE	
ROCK GROUP	

38

39   DATE:

NAME OF SPECIMEN: _____

TYPE OF SPECIMEN: _____

LOCATION: _____

LOCATION DESCRIPTION: _____

SPECIMEN DESCRIPTION: _____

PICTURE TAKEN ▨   SPECIMEN WRAPPED ▨

CATALOG NUMBER _____

PROPERTIES	NOTES
COLOR	
HARDNESS	
STREAK	
VISIBLE MINERALS	
GRAIN SIZE	
ROCK GROUP	

39

40   DATE:

NAME OF SPECIMEN: _____

TYPE OF SPECIMEN: _____

LOCATION: _____

LOCATION DESCRIPTION: _____

SPECIMEN DESCRIPTION: _____

PICTURE TAKEN ▪   SPECIMEN WRAPPED ▪

CATALOG NUMBER _____

PROPERTIES	NOTES
COLOR	
HARDNESS	
STREAK	
VISIBLE MINERALS	
GRAIN SIZE	
ROCK GROUP	

40

41 DATE:

NAME OF SPECIMEN: _____

TYPE OF SPECIMEN: _____

LOCATION: _____

LOCATION DESCRIPTION: _____

SPECIMEN DESCRIPTION: _____

PICTURE TAKEN ☐   SPECIMEN WRAPPED ☐

CATALOG NUMBER _____

PROPERTIES	NOTES
COLOR	
HARDNESS	
STREAK	
VISIBLE MINERALS	
GRAIN SIZE	
ROCK GROUP	

41

42 DATE:

NAME OF SPECIMEN: _____

TYPE OF SPECIMEN: _____

LOCATION: _____

LOCATION DESCRIPTION: _____

SPECIMEN DESCRIPTION: _____

PICTURE TAKEN ▦   SPECIMEN WRAPPED ▦

CATALOG NUMBER _____

PROPERTIES	NOTES
COLOR	
HARDNESS	
STREAK	
VISIBLE MINERALS	
GRAIN SIZE	
ROCK GROUP	

42

43 DATE:

NAME OF SPECIMEN: _____

TYPE OF SPECIMEN: _____

LOCATION: _____

LOCATION DESCRIPTION: _____

SPECIMEN DESCRIPTION: _____

PICTURE TAKEN ☐   SPECIMEN WRAPPED ☐

CATALOG NUMBER _____

PROPERTIES	NOTES
COLOR	
HARDNESS	
STREAK	
VISIBLE MINERALS	
GRAIN SIZE	
ROCK GROUP	

44 DATE:

NAME OF SPECIMEN: _____

TYPE OF SPECIMEN: _____

LOCATION: _____

LOCATION DESCRIPTION: _____

SPECIMEN DESCRIPTION: _____

PICTURE TAKEN ■ SPECIMEN WRAPPED ■

CATALOG NUMBER _____

PROPERTIES	NOTES
COLOR	
HARDNESS	
STREAK	
VISIBLE MINERALS	
GRAIN SIZE	
ROCK GROUP	

44

45   DATE:

NAME OF SPECIMEN: _____

TYPE OF SPECIMEN: _____

LOCATION: _____

LOCATION DESCRIPTION: _____

SPECIMEN DESCRIPTION: _____

PICTURE TAKEN ▢   SPECIMEN WRAPPED ▢

CATALOG NUMBER _____

PROPERTIES	NOTES
COLOR	
HARDNESS	
STREAK	
VISIBLE MINERALS	
GRAIN SIZE	
ROCK GROUP	

46   DATE:

NAME OF SPECIMEN: _____

TYPE OF SPECIMEN: _____

LOCATION: _____

LOCATION DESCRIPTION: _____

SPECIMEN DESCRIPTION: _____

PICTURE TAKEN ▪   SPECIMEN WRAPPED ▪

CATALOG NUMBER _____

PROPERTIES	NOTES
COLOR	
HARDNESS	
STREAK	
VISIBLE MINERALS	
GRAIN SIZE	
ROCK GROUP	

46

47   DATE:

NAME OF SPECIMEN: _____

TYPE OF SPECIMEN: _____

LOCATION: _____

LOCATION DESCRIPTION: _____

SPECIMEN DESCRIPTION: _____

PICTURE TAKEN ▪   SPECIMEN WRAPPED ▪

CATALOG NUMBER _____

PROPERTIES	NOTES
COLOR	
HARDNESS	
STREAK	
VISIBLE MINERALS	
GRAIN SIZE	
ROCK GROUP	

48 DATE:

NAME OF SPECIMEN: _____

TYPE OF SPECIMEN: _____

LOCATION: _____

LOCATION DESCRIPTION: _____

SPECIMEN DESCRIPTION: _____

PICTURE TAKEN ▩   SPECIMEN WRAPPED ▩

CATALOG NUMBER _____

PROPERTIES	NOTES
COLOR	
HARDNESS	
STREAK	
VISIBLE MINERALS	
GRAIN SIZE	
ROCK GROUP	

48

49 DATE:

NAME OF SPECIMEN: _____

TYPE OF SPECIMEN: _____

LOCATION: _____

LOCATION DESCRIPTION: _____

SPECIMEN DESCRIPTION: _____

PICTURE TAKEN ▨   SPECIMEN WRAPPED ▨

CATALOG NUMBER _____

PROPERTIES	NOTES
COLOR	
HARDNESS	
STREAK	
VISIBLE MINERALS	
GRAIN SIZE	
ROCK GROUP	

50

DATE:

NAME OF SPECIMEN: _____

TYPE OF SPECIMEN: _____

LOCATION: _____

LOCATION DESCRIPTION: _____

SPECIMEN DESCRIPTION: _____

PICTURE TAKEN ▪   SPECIMEN WRAPPED ▪

CATALOG NUMBER _____

PROPERTIES	NOTES
COLOR	
HARDNESS	
STREAK	
VISIBLE MINERALS	
GRAIN SIZE	
ROCK GROUP	

50

Good Luck, Rock Hounds!

Well, rock hounds, there you have it. Now you know everything you need to know to be a successful rock hound and treasure hunter! I hope this book travels with you on many adventures for years to come and that you never stop exploring mystery specimens in all kinds of interesting places—from right in your backyard to halfway across the world. This planet is full of treasures; go out there and find them!

Glossary

atom: The smallest building block of all things in the universe that can't be broken down into smaller parts by chemical reactions.

bedrock: A rock that is still in its original place and beneath the soil or other material that may be covering it at the surface.

chemical: A combination of atoms to form a substance, like a mineral. Everything is made up of chemicals.

chemistry: The study of chemicals and how they interact with each other.

cleavage: The way a mineral will break along weaknesses in its chemicals.

core: The center of the Earth.

crust: The outermost layer of the rocky part of the Earth.

crystal: A solid chemical in which atoms are arranged into a repeating pattern that forms a shape.

element: A substance made of atoms that all have exactly the same internal structure.

felsic igneous rock: A rock that has cooled from molten material that contains the mineral quartz.

fossil: The preserved remains of plants and animals found inside of rocks.

fracture: What a mineral does when broken against its cleavage.

gem or gemstone: A mineral that is cut and polished and used for making jewelry and ornaments.

geochemist: A person who studies the chemistry of rocks and minerals.

geologist: A person who studies rocks and minerals and how they form.

geology: The study of rocks and minerals and how they form.

habit: The way a mineral forms crystals.

igneous: Rocks that have formed from the cooling of molten rock material.

intermediate igneous rock: A rock that has cooled from molten material that contains a small amount of quartz.

lava: Molten rock that has made it onto the surface of the Earth.

luster: How a mineral looks in natural light. It normally is described to be like another object that people know—like "waxy" or "pearly" or "metallic."

mafic igneous rock: A rock that has cooled from molten material that does not contain the mineral quartz.

magma: Molten rock that is underground.

mantle: A very thick layer of the Earth between the crust and the core.

massive: When a mineral forms clumps.

metamorphic: Rocks that have minerals that have changed but did not melt after being heated and/or put under pressure.

metamorphism: A process that combines elements, such as melting, weathering, or cooking.

mine dump: Piles of waste rock that miners left behind when they were searching for minerals to sell.

minerals: Naturally occurring chemicals that make up the Earth's rocks.

molten: Liquid rock.

plate boundaries: The places where plates meet.

plates: Large slabs of the Earth's crust.

plutonic igneous rock: Coarse-grained rocks that have formed from the slow cooling of molten rock underground.

precious: A gemstone that is very rare.

rock cycle: The way rocks are formed, weathered, eroded, and melted or otherwise changed to form new rocks.

rock forming minerals: The major minerals that form the rocks of the Earth's crust.

rock hound: A person with a passion for collecting rocks and minerals who may not have studied them like geologists do.

rocks: Groups of minerals joined together to form clumps.

rot: To break down because of a change in chemicals over time as the chemicals react with air, water, or even other minerals.

sedimentary: Rocks made up of fragments of rocks or minerals from older, existing rocks.

sediment: Loose fragment of rock or mineral that has been transported by water, ice, or wind.

semiprecious: A gemstone that is not very rare.

specific gravity: A measure of how heavy a mineral is by how many grams are in one cubic centimeter.

specimen: A sample of rock or mineral you have collected.

streak: The color of a powdered mineral.

twinning: The way some minerals grow when one crystal grows next to and is joined to the same mineral. Sometimes many crystals grow this way to form multiple twins.

vein: A long, often thin layer of once-molten rock that has been squeezed into cracks of existing rocks and cooled.

volcanic igneous rock: A rock that forms when lava cools on the Earth's surface.

vug: A space inside a rock with crystals growing into the center.

Fact Sheets Index

A

Actinolite, 75
Agate, 108
Alabaster, 64
Amazonite, 76
Amber, 88
Amethyst, 87
Amphibole, 71
Amphibolite, 141
Andalusite, 108
Andesite, 128
Anorthoclase, 105
Anthracite, 139
Apatite, 74
Aquamarine, 82
Aragonite, 65
Arsenopyrite, 49
Augite, 95
Azurite, 83

B

Banded iron formation
   (BIF), 140
Barite, 64
Basalt, 130
Bauxite, 140
Beryl, 69
Biotite, 93
Bismuth, 59
Bornite, 87
Breccia, 133

C

Calcite, 101
Carbonatite, 125
Cassiterite, 110
Cerussite, 105
Chalcopyrite, 54
Chalk, 138
Chert, 136

Chlorite, 79
Chromite, 96
Cinnabar, 117
Citrine, 88
Conglomerate, 133
Copper, 58
Corundum, 111
Covellite, 83
Crocidolite, 84
Cummingtonite, 73
Cuprite, 114

D

Dacite, 130
Diamond, 91
Diatomite, 136
Diopside, 75
Diorite, 123
Dolomite, 65

E

Emerald, 77
Epidote, 78

F

Feldspar, 60
Flint, 109
Fluorite, 106

G

Gabbro, 124
Galena, 52
Garnet, 115
Gneiss, 141
Goethite, 112
Gold, 57
Granite, 120
Granodiorite, 122
Graphite, 97
Graywacke, 134
Gypsum, 62

H

Halite, 104
Hematite, 99
Herkimer diamond, 103
Hornblende, 95
Hornfels, 145

I

Ignimbrite, 126
Ilmenite, 97

J

Jadeite, 77
Jet, 96

K

Kaolinite, 63
Kyanite, 80

L

Labradorite, 81
Laterite, 138
Lignite, 139
Limestone, 137

M

Magnetite, 98
Malachite, 79
Marble, 144
Marcasite, 50
Mercury, 54
Mica, 61
Migmatite, 142
Milky quartz, 68
Molybdenite, 51
Monzonite, 121
Muscovite, 103

N

Nephrite, 76

O

Obsidian, 132
Oil shale, 134
Olivine, 70
Oolite, 137

Opal, 67
Orthoclase, 86

P

Pegmatite, 121
Peridotite, 124
Phyllite, 146
Picrite, 125
Plagioclase, 68
Platinum, 53
Porphyry, 122
Pumice, 131
Pyrite, 55
Pyroclastic, 127
Pyrolusite, 98
Pyroxene, 72
Pyrrhotite, 56

Q

Quartz, 100
Quartzite, 145

R

Realgar, 116
Rhodochrosite, 85
Rhyolite, 131
Rose quartz, 85
Ruby, 116
Rutile, 113

S

Sandstone, 135
Sapphire, 82
Schist, 143
Scoria, 127
Selenite, 102
Serpentinite, 147
Shale, 135
Siderite, 89
Sillimanite, 69
Silver, 48
Slate, 146
Smoky quartz, 110
Soapstone, 147
Sodalite, 81
Sphalerite, 112

Staurolite, 111
Stibnite, 52
Sulfur, 92
Syenite, 123

T

Talc, 73
Tiger's eye, 107
Titanite, 114
Tonalite, 120
Topaz, 90
Tourmaline, 94
Trachyte, 128

Tremolite, 66
Tuff, 129
Turquoise, 84

U

Ulexite, 104

W

Wolframite, 53
Wollastonite, 66

Z

Zircon, 115

Index

B

Blows, 16

C

Carbonates and friends, 15
    alabaster, 64
    apatite, 74
    aragonite, 65
    azurite, 83
    calcite, 101
    carbonatite, 125
    cerussite, 105
    dolomite, 65
    gypsum, 62
    malachite, 79
    rhodochrosite, 85
    selenite, 102
    siderite, 89
    turquoise, 84
Chains, 14
Chemical composition, 6, 10
Chemicals, 2
Chemical weathering, 20
Chemistry, 2
Cleaning specimens, 37–38
Cleavage, 9
Coal
    anthracite, 139
    lignite, 139
Coal macerals
    jet, 96
Collections, organizing, 43–45
Color
    fact sheet symbols, 33
    of minerals, 8
    of rocks, 21–22
    streak, 33
Core, of the earth, 5
Crust, 4–5
Crystal habits, 10

D

Devils Tower, WY, 28
Double blocks, 14

E

Earth, layers of, 4–5
Elements, 2
    in mineral formation, 7
    periodic table, 12–13

F

Fact sheets
    colored tabs, 32
    organization of rocks and
        minerals, 34–35
    reading, 31
    symbols, 33, 43
Felsic igneous rocks, 25
    granite, 120
    ignimbrite, 126
    monzonite, 121
    obsidian, 132
    pegmatite, 121
    porphyry, 122
    pumice, 131
    pyroclastic, 127
    rhyolite, 131
    scoria, 127
    tonalite, 120
    tuff, 129
Field notebook, 31, 149
    catalog number, 150–151
    colored tabs, 32, 42
    date, 151
    how to use, 150–153
    location, 152
    location description, 152
    name of specimen, 151
    picture taken, 153
    properties table, 153

specimen description, 152
specimen wrapped, 153
type of specimen, 151
Fool's gold, 17, 55
Fossils, 17
Fracture, 9
Framework, 14

G

Gemologists, 3
Gemstones, 15
amazonite, 76
amethyst, 87
aquamarine, 82
cassiterite, 110
cuprite, 114
diamond, 91
diopside, 75
emerald, 77
garnet, 115
jadeite, 77
jet, 96
nephrite, 76
opal, 67
ruby, 116
sapphire, 82
topaz, 90
turquoise, 84
Geochemists, 3
Geodes, 16–17
Geologists, ix, 3
Geology, 3
Gold, 17
Grain size, 22, 33–34, 41–42
Grand Canyon, AZ, 28

H

Habits, 10
Hardness
making your own
scale, 36–37
of minerals, 8–9
of rocks, 22

I

Identification (ID)
cleaning specimens, 37–38
steps for minerals, 38–40
steps for rocks, 40–43
supplies, 35–36
testing hardness, 36–37
Igneous rocks, 4, 18, 23–24
andesite, 128
basalt, 130
carbonatite, 125
dacite, 130
diorite, 123
felsic, 25
gabbro, 124
granite, 120
granodiorite, 122
identifying, 40–41
ignimbrite, 126
intermediate, 25
mafic, 25
monzonite, 121
obsidian, 132
pegmatite, 121
peridotite, 124
picrite, 125
plutonic, 23
porphyry, 122
pumice, 131
pyroclastic, 127
rhyolite, 131
scoria, 127
syenite, 123
tonalite, 120
trachyte, 128
tuff, 129
volcanic, 23–24
Inorganic, 6
Intermediate igneous rocks, 25
andesite, 128
dacite, 130
diorite, 123
granodiorite, 122
ignimbrite, 126
syenite, 123
trachyte, 128

L

Lava, 23–24
Luster, 8

M

Mafic igneous rocks, 25
  basalt, 130
  gabbro, 124
  peridotite, 124
  picrite, 125
  pyroclastic, 127
  scoria, 127
  tuff, 129
Magma, 23
Mantle, 4
Massive, 10
Mechanical weathering, 20
Metamorphic rocks, 4, 18, 25
  amphibolite, 141
  gneiss, 141
  hornfels, 145
  identifying, 40–41
  marble, 144
  migmatite, 142
  phyllite, 146
  quartzite, 145
  schist, 143
  serpentinite, 147
  slate, 146
  soapstone, 147
Metamorphism, 7
Mineralogists, 3
Minerals
  carbonates and friends, 15
  chemical composition, 10
  cleavage, 9
  as coatings on other
    minerals, 16
  color, 8
  crystal habits, 10
  definition, 6
  fact sheet
    organization, 34–35
  fact sheet symbols, 32–34
  fool's gold, 17
  formation of, 7

fossils replaced by, 17
fracture, 9
gemstones, 15
geodes, 16–17
groups, 11
hardness, 8–9
identifying, 38–40
luster, 8
native elements, 11
oxides and friends, 11, 15
properties of, 7–10
quartz, 16
silicates, 11, 14
specific gravity, 10
streak, 10
sulfides and friends, 11
vugs, 16
Mohs Scale of Hardness,
  8–9, 36–37
Molten rock, 4, 23
Mt. St. Helens, WA, 28

N

Native elements, 11
  bismuth, 59
  copper, 58
  diamond, 91
  gold, 17, 57
  graphite, 97
  mercury, 54
  platinum, 53
  silver, 48
  sulfur, 92
Naturally occurring, 6

O

Origin, rock, 22
Oxides and friends, 11, 15
  cassiterite, 110
  chromite, 96
  corundum, 111
  cuprite, 114
  fluorite, 106
  goethite, 112
  halite, 104
  hematite, 99

ilmenite, 97
magnetite, 98
pyrolusite, 98
ruby, 116
rutile, 113
sapphire, 82
ulexite, 104
wolframite, 53

P

Periodic table of
elements, 12–13
Plate boundaries, 5
Plates, 5
Plutonic igneous rocks, 23
carbonatite, 125
diorite, 123
gabbro, 124
granite, 120
granodiorite, 122
monzonite, 121
pegmatite, 121
peridotite, 124
porphyry, 122
syenite, 123
tonalite, 120
Porphyries, 21
Precious gemstones, 15
Properties, mineral, 7–10
chemical composition, 10
cleavage, 9
color, 8
crystal habits, 10
fracture, 9
hardness, 8–9
luster, 8
specific gravity, 10
streak, 10

Q

Quartz, 16

R

Rings, 14
Rock cycle, 18–19
Rock hound kits, 30

Rock hounds, ix, 27
Rock hunting, 29
Rocks
characteristics of, 19–22
classification, 21
color, 21–22
composition, 21
definition, 18
fact sheet
organization, 34–35
fact sheet symbols, 32–34
grain size, 22
groups, 4, 18, 23–25, 33
hardness, 22
identifying, 40–43
igneous, 4, 18, 23–24
metamorphic, 4, 18, 25
origin, 22
porphyries, 21
sedimentary, 4, 18, 25
Rotting, 20

S

Sedimentary rocks, 4, 18, 25
anthracite, 139
banded iron formation
(BIF), 140
bauxite, 140
chalk, 138
chert, 136
conglomerate, 133
diatomite, 136
graywacke, 134
identifying, 40–41
laterite, 138
lignite, 139
limestone, 137
oil shale, 134
oolite, 137
sandstone, 135
shale, 135
Semi-precious gemstones, 15
Sheets, 14
Silicates, 11, 14, 16, 100
actinolite, 75
agate, 108

Silicates (*continued*)
amazonite, 76
amethyst, 87
amphibole, 71
andalusite, 108
anorthoclase, 105
aquamarine, 82
augite, 95
beryl, 69
biotite, 93
chlorite, 79
citrine, 88
crocidolite, 84
cummingtonite, 73
diopside, 75
emerald, 77
epidote, 78
feldspar, 60
flint, 109
garnet, 115
Herkimer diamond, 103
hornblende, 95
jadeite, 77
kaolinite, 63
kyanite, 80
labradorite, 81
mica, 61
milky quartz, 68
muscovite, 103
nephrite, 76
olivine, 70
opal, 67
orthoclase, 86
plagioclase, 68
pyroxene, 72
rose quartz, 85
sillimanite, 69
smoky quartz, 110
sodalite, 81
staurolite, 111
talc, 73
tiger's eye, 107
titanite, 114
topaz, 90
tourmaline, 94
tremolite, 66
wollastonite, 66
zircon, 115
Single blocks, 14
Solid, 6
Specific gravity, 10
Specimens, 5
Streak, 10, 33
Streak test, 39
Sulfides and friends, 11
arsenopyrite, 49
barite, 64
bornite, 87
chalcopyrite, 54
cinnabar, 117
covellite, 83
galena, 52
marcasite, 50
molybdenite, 51
pyrite, 55
pyrrhotite, 56
realgar, 116
sphalerite, 112
stibnite, 52
Supplies, 30, 35–36

T
Twinning, 10

V
Veins, 16
Volcanic igneous rocks, 24
andesite, 128
basalt, 130
dacite, 130
ignimbrite, 126
obsidian, 132
picrite, 125
pumice, 131
pyroclastic, 127
rhyolite, 131
scoria, 127
trachyte, 128
tuff, 129
Vugs, 16–17

W
Weathering, 20

Acknowledgments

Books like this are written because we stand on the shoulders of the giants of geology who came before us. I thank them for their perseverance, wisdom, and passion, and hope that I can do them proud by spreading the joy of rock and mineral collecting to the young.

About the Author

GARY LEWIS grew up in Sydney, Australia, where he fell in love with rock and mineral collecting after many holidays on the coast with family and gold-panning trips with his beloved grandfather "Pop" Wilson. After school, Gary trained as a geologist at Sydney University and then worked as a high school teacher in a rural school. He then moved to working in education programs for government agencies such as the Commonwealth Scientific and Industrial Research Organisation and started up a geology education program at Geoscience Australia—the nation's geological survey.

In 2003 Gary moved to the United States to become the director of education and outreach for the Geological Society of America. In 2015 he started his own education company, GEOetc.com, which aims to bring the excitement of geology to the public and runs trips to Hawaii, Iceland, Australia, Europe, and beyond. He is also the author of more than 25 teacher resources and books on Hawaiian volcanoes, plate tectonics, and even homesteading.

He was the founding member and chair of the commission on geoscience education, training, and technology transfer for the International Union of Geological Sciences.

Gary is still collecting rocks and minerals and is lucky to live in Maine, where he is surrounded by amazing collecting locations and has even collected minerals on his gravel driveway. He collects whenever he travels and has rocks displayed around his house on windowsills and bookcases.

Gary can often be found talking to school students about volcanoes, earthquakes, and plate tectonics, as his passion for everyone to understand the Earth is limitless.

Gary lives on a small farm with his wife and youngest children, dog, cat, horse, and rooster.

CPSIA information can be obtained
at www.ICGtesting.com
Printed in the USA
BVHW091346131119
563602BV00002B/2/P